Boston

Boston

Text by Marilyn Wood
Updated by: Natasha Babaian
Edited by Media Content Marketing, Inc.
Photography: Chris Coe except pages 4, 5, 19, 32, 58, 63, 64, 67, 72, 82 by Jon Davison
Cover photograph by Chris Coe
*Photo Editor:*Naomi Zinn
Layout: Media Content Marketing, Inc.
Cartography by Ortelius Design
Managing Editor: Tony Halliday

Sixth Edition 2002 (Reprinted 2004, twice)

Contacting the Editors

Every effort has been made to provide accurate information in this publication, but changes are inevitable. The publisher cannot be responsible for any resulting loss, inconvenience or injury. We would appreciate it if readers would call our attention to any errors or outdated information by contacting Berlitz Publishing, PO Box 7910, London SE1 1WE, England. Fax: (44) 20 7403 0290;
e-mail: berlitz@apaguide.co.uk; www.berlitzpublishing.com

Printed in Singapore by Insight Print Services (Pte) Ltd, 38 Joo Koon Road, Singapore 628990. Tel: (65) 6865-1600. Fax: (65) 6861-6438

030/406 RP

CONTENTS

• A ☛ in the text denotes a highly recommended sight

Boston

BOSTON AND THE BOSTONIANS

Boston, the City on a Hill, the Hub of the Universe, the Cradle of the Revolution, the place where Boston Brahmins congregate on Beacon Hill, the source of Boston beans, Boston cod, and Boston cream pie, the home of the cliff-hanging Boston Red Sox—these are all common Boston associations. They're still appropriate enough, but Boston is also modern and forward-looking, gearing up for the next century. Her universities are turning out students that are founding advanced technology companies in the hundreds and making New England rich once again, but what every visitor will notice immediately is something else: Sheetrock walls and re-routed sidewalks are everywhere, massive machinery lurches and roars lifting up huge mounds of earth. Crowds of hard hats are ripping up downtown. They are all participating in the "Big Dig" to put the city back together again by re-routing the Interstate underneath the city instead of above it. Boston is being made whole again. When this $11-billion project that began in 1991 is finished in 2004, Boston's waterfront and North End will be reunited with downtown.

Boston is a port city. There's a tang in the air, a scent of the sea. Much of its wealth came from the humble cod that were fished off the Grand Banks, which is why you'll find the wooden Sacred Cod hanging in the Massachusetts state house. Trade followed and built more wealth. Yet it's a cultured city, one of the most cultured in the United States with an enormous number of classical musical groups in particular. Unlike New York, Boston wasn't founded to make money, it was founded as a City on a Hill, a beacon of righteousness to others. And although it may have persecuted some in that name, it remained

Picture-perfect Harvard Yard — the oldest part of the famous university.

a beacon of intellectual light in the 19th-century, which is why Oliver Wendell Holmes felt justified in dubbing the State House the "Hub of the Solar System." Bostonians in typical style took it a step further and substituted the phrase the Hub of the Universe, a misquote that has stuck. Certainly back then Boston was a leading intellectual center. Many Bostonians were calling for the abolition of slavery and were demanding rights and suffrage for women. Today you can follow in the footsteps of those who founded the Anti Slavery Society and who worked for women's rights by taking the Black Heritage Trail and the Women's Heritage Trail.

The trail that started it all though is the Freedom Trail, a route that links sixteen of the sites associated with one of the most influential events of the 18th-century, the American Revolution. It's a story that never palls—the uprising of brilliant and brave men against tyranny. Visit the places where they railed against the Stamp Acts, see where the first martyrs fell, and go aboard the ship that triumphed against the British in the "second revolution" of 1812.

The figures still live in our hearts and minds as we walk the Freedom Trail sitting before the pulpits in which they challenged the authorities, seeing the tower where the two lanterns were hung, or standing at their gravesides. Sam Adams, Thomas Paine, John Hancock, Paul Revere, Robert Treat Paine: They are all here, surrounded by their legacy.

History is in Boston. It has an Old World flavor to it, more than most cities on the East Coast, except perhaps for Philadelphia. The downtown streets are not laid out in a traditional grid. They are labrynthine, giving it the appearance and feel more of London than New York. The buildings downtown though present a wonderful amalgam of past and present. New modern buildings have been built with a concern for their location and that of the buildings that surround them so that there is a harmony to the skyline. The visual synthesis of old red brick and new glass towers set against winter snow, spring magnolia blossoms, or the vibrant and kaleidoscopic colors of the fall are what make the city so pleasing to the eye. Boston's prime glory is its past, and it is this rich history that first draws visitors, but it is far from being Boston's sole attribute. Within just a few square miles boats roar across the harbor, planes swoop across the water, and seagulls glide around high-rise towers that dwarf the old colonial meeting houses below.

The people who built the city came from all over the world, and the patchwork of neighborhoods they created survives to this day. The Puritans were first in 1630 and they built many of the steepled churches that were modeled on those by Christopher Wren. They and the generations who came after them gave the city its reputation for Yankee thrift and practicality, its penchant for private clubs, and its passion for privacy and decorum. The blacks, many of whom were artisans, lived on the North Side of Beacon Hill. The Irish, who fled oppression and starvation in the 19th-century, came to work in the homes of the wealthy and worked their way up in society becoming super-successful in politics as did the Fitzgeralds and Kennedys, for example. The Italians who came to work in the maritime trades established themselves in the North End where many of them still are. The neighborhoods that they created are still distinct today. Beacon Hill is still the home of many professionals and descendants of the Boston Brahmins who lived there. Italians still live in the North End and sit out on the street just as they might if they were still living in the villages around Naples. The Chinese and other Asian immigrants are still clustered in tiny Chinatown. The Irish are still in South Boston. They have all managed to retain a strong sense of identity and community.

The huge student population only adds more flavor to the stew. Harvard, MIT, Tufts, Boston University, Boston College, the University of Massachusetts are all located here (a total of 32 colleges in Boston proper). Every year in September 90,000 to 135,000 students descend on the city; they seem to be unloading their U-hauls on every corner. Harvard and MIT (Massachusetts Institute of Technology) lie just "across the river," dominating the city of Cambridge. Visitors often think of Cambridge as an extension of the Hub, but it is actually an independent city, even though it's only a short subway ride away. Bostonians see their academic neighbors as head-in-the-clouds types, and because of the locals' left-of-center tendencies, Cambridge is sometimes called the "People's Republic of Cambridge."

Thanks largely to the student population, there's enough entertainment for a much bigger city. People corner you to tell you about their favorite restaurant or bar, and popular haunts are packed most nights. The long drawl of the upper class "brahmin" (sounding not unlike a contrived English accent) resonates in smart restaurants and tearooms. Pints of Guinness and sing-alongs are the order of the day in the Irish pubs, and you would be hard pressed to find a seat in the city's best seafood restaurants.

It's also a sports-crazy town. The city's very well being seems wedded to the success of its various major league teams. When the Red Sox baseball team is on a winning streak, the headlines read "Ten games that shook the Hub," and columnists talk of a "Summer to smile about and enjoy." In every bar in town the television is tuned in when a home team is playing, and chat dries up for couples out for a romantic dinner.

Yet however worldly Boston may appear, it still has the appealing quality of a network of small villages and neighborhoods. Enjoy its little quirks and understated sophistication and it won't be long before you feel as much at home as the locals themselves.

Set your sails for the Charles River — where visitors and natives alike can escape the traffic of urban existence.

A BRIEF HISTORY

Beginnings

The Algonquin Indians called the peninsula on which Boston stands Shawmut. In 1624, William Blackstone became the first white settler. A recluse, he settled on Shawmut with a good stock of books and a bull. In 1630, he invited some neighbors from Charlestown to join him on what is now Boston Common.

Like the Pilgrims who had put down roots several years previously in Plymouth, these neighbors were religious refugees from a small Lincolnshire town in England called Boston. They had fled their homeland to avoid the persecution meted out by Anglican Bishop Laud to the Dissenters.

The group, which was called the Massachusetts Bay Company and was led by John Winthrop, had brought its own royal charter to the New World, a document which effectively authorized self-rule. The small community grew fast, and, with its excellent natural harbor, prospered as a trading port, exporting cod to Europe. In 1632 Boston became the capital of the Massachusetts Bay Colony. The colony operated under a strict Puritan ethical code, which brooked no opposition. For some it was too strict, and they were either driven out or left of their own accord, like Blackstone himself, who moved to Rhode Island.

A Question of Tax

Charles II ascended the English throne in 1660, reinstating the Navigation Acts in that same year. These insisted that colonial trade be carried out solely with England, implementing a form of trade protectionism. Royal authority was further reinforced when the initial charter of the Massachusetts Bay Company was rescinded in 1684, and New England made a royal colony. Two years later, James II appointed the despotic Sir Edmund Andros as the royal governor of the Province of Massachusetts. His rule was short-lived, however, for when James II was deposed in 1689 in the Glorious Revolution, Andros was booted out, too.

Walking the Freedom Trail — tour colonial and revolutionary sites en route to Bunker Hill.

In the first half of the 18th century, Boston continued to grow, becoming the largest city in North America. Maritime trade flourished, and many wharves had been built along the waterfront. The wealthy merchants started to challenge the Puritan ministers' leadership. Evidence of their growing power and wealth can be seen today in such buildings as Faneuil Hall and Quincy Market. George III noted the colony's prosperity and having emptied the English treasury during the Seven Years War with France (1756 to 1763), the British monarch turned to the New World. He introduced a series of taxes, the Revenue or Sugar Act in 1764 (imposing duties on silk, .wine, and sugar), and the Stamp Act in 1765, levying a tax on all publications. These measures angered the colonists and crowds rioted in Boston.

Discontent grew, and soon groups of protesters were meeting together to discuss the situation. The most active group was the Sons of Liberty, which numbered among its members wealthy merchant John Hancock, silversmith Paul Revere, and orator-pamphleteer Samuel Adams, who was a Harvard graduate. Their rallying cry, "No taxation without representation," echoed belligerently throughout Boston and the colony. When the Townshend Acts were introduced in 1767, taxing lead, paper, and the colonists' favorite drink, tea, resentment increased further. Troops were sent to occupy Boston and restore order, but tension remained high, and many a fracas occurred between redcoat British soldiers and locals. On 5 March 1770, locals were taunting a British officer. He used the butt of his rifle

The Jack-of-All-Trades Patriot

Paul Revere is Boston's best loved son, due to his exploits on the night of 18 April 1775, immortalized in Henry Wadsworth Longfellow's *Paul Revere's Ride*:

Listen, my children, and you shall hear
Of the midnight ride of Paul Revere,
On the eighteenth of April, in Seventy-Five ...
He said to his friend, "If the British march
By land or sea from the town tonight,
Hang a lantern aloft in the belfry arch
Of the North Church tower as a signal light —
One, if by land, and two, if by sea...."

It doesn't matter that Revere did not in fact reach Concord and was in fact captured by the British on his way from Lexington. Revere often acted as a messenger for the Sons of Liberty and he was also a first-class propagandist for the cause, making provocative engravings, such as the famous one depicting the Boston Massacre. He was known primarily as a craftsman, however, and notably as a silversmith, but he also turned his hand to being a lieutenant colonel of artillery, a copper roller, bell ringer, and dentist, while somehow finding time to sire 16 children from two wives. He died in 1818, aged 83.

to push them away and a scuffle ensued. When the fighting stopped the Redcoats had killed five people including Crispus Attucks, a black man who was the first to fall in the American Revolution. This attack gave the cause its first martyrs, and the incident became renowned as the Boston Massacre.

England continued to try to restrain American trade, and in 1773, the Government passed the Tea Act, which subsidized the East India Company's tea at the expense of colonial merchants. The colonials refused to pay the tax on tea, and after rounds of fruitless negotiations with the governor, on 16 December Samuel Adams proclaimed to the crowds at the Old South Meeting House: "Gentlemen, this meeting can do nothing more to save the country."

A thousand demonstrators left the Old South and went down to Griffin's Wharf, where, led by the Sons of Liberty, they boarded three vessels and dumped 342 chests of tea into the harbor. In response to this brazen act of defiance the British dissolved local government and closed the harbor. The edicts announcing these actions were dubbed the Intolerable Acts. Armed confrontation now seemed inevitable.

War

The colonists began stockpiling arms and ammunitions. In April 1775, military governor General Thomas Gage suspecting that the colonists had amassed a cache of arms in Concord, 18 miles (30 km) northwest of Boston, planned to seize it. What took place next is the stuff of legends.

Paul Revere rode to Lexington where he met John Hancock and Samuel Adams, then continued on to Concord with Samuel Prescott and William Dawes. They were ambushed, but Prescott managed to complete the journey to warn the Minutemen of the English troops' arrival.

War broke out the next day, 19 April 1775. The redcoats killed several Minutemen on Lexington Green; there were casualties on both sides at North Bridge, and more fighting ensued as the English troops retreated to Boston. On that first day, a total of 73 British and 49 colonists died. In the following weeks, colonists flooded into towns surrounding Boston to besiege the city.

On 17 June General Gage attempted to break the blockade in "the first great battle of the Revolution." It was fought at Breed's Hill in Charlestown, where the colonists had set up a redoubt, but due to a geographical confusion, it is now known as the Battle of Bunker Hill).

The English underestimated the resolve of the rebels, and although they officially won the battle, they suffered terrible losses, with more than 1,000 men killed or wounded. The siege of Boston continued into the following year, under the command of General George Washington who pounded the city with artillery from his position on Dorchester Heights. Exhausted from the assault and lacking supplies, the British were forced to leave on what is now called Evacuation Day (17 March 1776). The war continued until 1783, but Boston itself was spared from further direct involvement.

The Paul Revere House on North Square is the oldest building in Boston.

Brahmins and Landfill

Maritime trade boomed after the Revolution, and industrial manufacturing flourished. Boston society centered on upper class merchants and industrialists, who had reputations for temperance, sobriety, and high self-esteem. Consequently they were referred to as "brahmins," after the Hindu caste that sets high moral standards.

The brahmins also valued culture, and the 19th century saw the founding of an array of Boston cultural institutions, so many in fact that Boston was dubbed "The Athens of America," with writers like Henry Wadsworth Longfellow at the forefront of a renaissance in philosophical and literary thought. The city was a significant center in the campaign for the abolition of slavery, as well as a stop on the so-called "Underground Railroad" for smuggling slaves into Canada.

Charles Dickens visited in 1842, the same year that Longfellow's *Poems on Slavery* appeared. Dickens described Boston in his *American Notes*, remarking that "the air was so clear, the houses were so bright and gay; … the gilded letters were so very golden; the bricks were so very red, the stone was so very white; … the knobs and plates upon the street doors so very marvelously bright and twinkling." His favorable impression was thanks largely to the efforts of one man, architect Charles Bulfinch (1763–1844). In starting a craze for Boston's distinctive, redbrick Georgian-style buildings, he gave the city something of a facelift.

The city's prosperity also fostered expansion. Prior to the Revolution, Boston's topography was far from impressive: a seemingly precarious peninsula on the end of a thin neck of land, with foul mud flats on either side. During the 1800s Boston's area tripled. The tops of the three original hills on which the city stood were lopped off, and the earth was used to extend the shoreline and fill in the marshes. Faneuil Hall Marketplace, the South End, Bay Village, and Back Bay are all the result of landfill projects. It took some 30 years, from 1857, to complete Back Bay, with trains importing wagonloads of gravel daily. The Victorian wonderland became a symbol of the city's prosperity and status.

Immigrants

The rapid increase in the city's population was one reason for the physical expansion. Immigrants were pouring in from Ireland, fleeing starvation caused by the Great Potato Famine (1845–50). They lived in poor conditions in tenements in the North and West End, and were often persecuted because they were Roman Catholics. In the late 19th-century many of the Irish had succeeded in establishing themselves and as they moved out of the congested slum areas, new waves of Italian and Eastern European immigrants arrived.

The Irish had a natural flair and predilection for politics. Since 1885, when the first Irish mayor was appointed, few years have passed when an Emerald Isle descendant has not held the office. In the first half of this century, political life was dominated by John F. Fitzgerald ("Honey Fitz"), grandfather of the late President John Fitzgerald Kennedy, and James Michael Curley, who was mayor four times. Raised in poor neighborhoods, the Irish were people's champions (even though Curley spent part of his fourth term in jail for fraud).

Renew or Recycle?

Ever since the Industrial Revolution, Boston has found itself increasingly overshadowed by New York in economic preeminence, and has suffered a gradual decline. In an attempt to revitalize the city, a massive urban renewal program was undertaken in the 1950s and 1960s, creating the Prudential Center in Back Bay and Government Center downtown. The most controversial renewal project, though, was the creation of the John Fitzgerald Expressway, which destroyed the West End and split the North End and the waterfront from the rest of the city. The current Big Dig is meant to fix this by re-routing the Expressway underneath the city.

The Minutemen Memorial — a vivid reminder of the cost of American freedom.

A different urban planning philosophy now prevails. More than 7,000 city buildings have been designated Historic Landmarks, and new uses have been found for old buildings: the former Natural History Museum is now a clothes store; Quincy Market has become Faneuil Hall Marketplace; and the naval yard and wharves have been transformed into offices and apartments. Post-war Boston was a commercial backwater. Then, in the 1980s, the city reinvented itself again with the help of MIT and other academic institutions, which led a boom in high technology — a development that has since become known as the "Massachusetts Miracle." The boom continues today and the results can be seen in the current construction and development.

Historical Landmarks

1630 Boston is founded by the Massachusetts Bay Company.

1635 Boston Latin, the country's first public school, is founded.

1636 Harvard University is founded.

1765 The Stamp Act is introduced. Riots follow.

1770 Five patriots killed in the Boston Massacre, 5 March.

1773 Boston Tea Party, 16 December.

1775 The War of American Independence begins on 19 April with skirmishes in Lexington and Concord.

1776 English troops retreat on Evacuation Day, 17 March.

1797 *U.S.S. Constitution* ("Old Ironsides") is launched.

1831 William Lloyd Garrison publishes the first edition of the abolitionist newspaper, *The Liberator*.

1857 Back Bay landfill project begins.

1872 Fire destroys 765 buildings in the Downtown area.

1875 Birth of the telephone: Alexander Graham Bell transmits the sound of speech along a wire.

1879 Mary Baker Eddy founds the Christian Science movement.

1918 Red Sox win their last World Series title.

1919 A tidal wave of molasses in the North End kills 21.

1960 Massachusetts senator John F. Kennedy is elected president.

1974 Buses are used to integrate predominantly black and white school districts; riots follow.

1983 Sitcom *Cheers* is first broadcast; greater renown follows.

1991 The mammoth Third Harbor Tunnel/Central Artery Project (better known by its popular moniker 'The Big Dig') begins.

1995 Boston Garden closes; Celtics and other teams move to FleetCenter.

1998 Massachusetts State House celebrates its 200th anniversary

2001 Two passenger airliners hijacked from Logan Airport by terrorists are crashed into New York's World Trade Center, killing nearly 3,000 people.

WHERE TO GO

Boston is so compact that it's perfect for walking. You can stroll through Downtown in an hour and explore a number of distinct neighborhoods: the cobbled lanes of Beacon Hill, the jumble of streets in the financial district, or the Victorian avenues of Back Bay. To get your bearings, take a run trolley ride and on and off as you go. If you have limited time, you may want to stick to the Freedom Trail, but otherwise get out and explore the neighborhoods. (Details of the main sights are given on page 41.)

BOSTON COMMON, BEACON HILL, AND THE ESPLANADE

Boston Common

The oldest public park in the United States the Common is Boston's historical, spiritual, and geographical heart. First settler William Blackstone sold the 48-acre (19-hectare) parcel of land to Boston residents in 1634. It served variously as a cow pasture (until 1830), drill field, and meeting place. During the Revolution the British regulars camped here. The stocks also stood here and many were hanged on the gallows too.

The copper-roofed **Park Street Station,** which was built in 1897, stands at one corner of the Common and is the country's oldest subway station.

Today Bostonians inevitably seem to wind up on the Common. Businesspeople stride along the red brick paths, office workers enjoy a picnic lunch, the elderly sun themselves on park benches, students read, and people gather by the bandstand and the Civil War Soldiers and Sailors

The gilded dome of the Massachusetts State House — a testament to US history.

Monument. On a hot day, kids play under the fountain at the **Frog Pond** (without frogs nowadays and once said to be a place for dunking witches). As evening approaches, tennis, volleyball, and softball get going. The adjacent **Public Garden** is far prettier than the Common. Still supported entirely by private donations, the country's original botanical garden boasts a wonderful selection of ornamental flowerbeds, rare trees, and lush lawns. Weeping willows hang over the lagoon, around which, in summer, you can take a soporific little tour on a Swan Boat, pedaled by a strapping young man or woman sitting at the rear. In winter, hardy skaters replace the swans. The garden's quirky sculptures and little fountains merit exploration. The most beguiling is the bronze Mrs. Mallard followed by her eight ducklings (near the Charles and Beacon Street entrance), a tribute to Robert McCloskey's *Make Way for Ducklings*, a famous children's tale (on sale in all local bookshops). It relates the traumas of rearing a family of ducklings in Boston.

The gilded dome of the **Massachusetts State House** glistens above the trees at the northern corner of the Common. Paul Revere and Sam Adams laid the cornerstone in 1785. Charles Bulfinch, architect of the US Capitol, designed the original core which was completed in 1798. In front of the neoclassical façade stand several statues including Anne Hutchinson, who left the intolerant colony for Rhode Island, Quaker Mary Dyer who was hung for her unorthodox views, and John F. Kennedy striding in front of the western wing.

Inside, history is expressed everywhere. Doric Hall displays portraits and statues of Abraham Lincoln and John Adams. Murals of Revolutionary events line Nurses' Hall, which features a moving sculpture of a nurse ministering to a wounded soldier during the Civil War. The heart of the building lies upstairs in the House of Representatives Chamber in which the "sacred cod" hangs as it has since 1784, a reminder of the city's humble beginnings as a fishing port. Opposite, the impressive domed Senate Chamber is lined with busts of Lafayette, Washington, and others.

A Sitcom Shrine

One of Boston's most popular attractions for visitors remains the Bull and Finch Pub (84 Beacon Street; Tel: 227-9605) – a wordplay on the city's best-known architect – though it remains better known as Cheers. It was once a typical neighborhood hangout until a couple of Hollywood producers dropped in well over a decade ago and decided to make what turned out to be a fantastically successful series based on the bar. Long-time regulars speak of now and the time BC, "Before Cheers." The studio set differed from the actual bar, and the atmosphere is markedly different from that of the show.

The bar is very crowded all year round. The quietest time to visit is about 4pm, but even then no one is likely to know your name.

Beacon Hill

Behind the State House, Boston's most desirable residential neighborhood has the air of a somnolent village, insulated from the traffic and vulgarity of the 20th century. It's still a preserve of the old-monied who occupy the Federal, Georgian, Greek Revival, and Victorian homes that have stoops, boot-scrapers, and wrought iron railings.

In the 19th century so many leading intellectuals lived here that the city became known as "The Athens of the United States." On **Chestnut Street** alone, there lived historian Francis Parkman, actor Edwin Booth, author Julia Ward Howe, and painter John Singer Sargent. Louisa May Alcott and Nathaniel Hawthorne resided on **Pinckney Street,** while **Beacon Street** which Oliver Wendell Holmes dubbed "the sunny street that holds the sifted few" boasted historian William Prescott. At number 10 Beacon, stop at the **Boston Athenaeum** (Tel. 227-0270; guided tours Tuesday and Thursday at 3pm; reservations needed), a haven for writers and intellectuals since it was established in 1807. The 750,000-volume collection is amazing, but so too is the interior of the 1849 building, which is exquisitely furnished with

Louisburg Square — hot property in Boston's exclusive Beacon Hill.

antiques, busts of Benjamin Franklin, Daniel Webster, and others, and several paintings by John Singer Sargent and Gilbert Stuart. Farther along Beacon at number 45, Harrison Gray Otis died in the house that Bulfinch designed for him. Don't miss the London-style **Louisburg Square** surrounded by some of the finest Greek Revival homes in New England.

Nichols House (55 Mount Vernon Street; Tel. 227-6993, open for guided tours May–October Tuesday–Saturday, noon–5pm; February–April and November–December Monday, Wednesday, and Friday noon–5pm), offers a chance to view the interior of a residence attributed to Bulfinch. The rooms are exactly as they were when the owner, Rose Standish Nichols, a noted landscape architect died in 1960. Furnishings include Flemish tapestries, Oriental rugs, and European and Asian art. Don't overlook **Acorn Street** — the prettiest of them all — a cobbled lane so narrow that cars can't park here to spoil a photographer's picture. **Charles Street** serves as the community's main street and as a magnet for serious antique collectors. Also note the Charles Street Meeting House, where Harriet Tubman, Sojourner Truth, and other abolitionists preached.

Head down Joy Street to the **African Meeting House** (see page 34) and to 141 Cambridge Street for the **Harrison Gray Otis House** (Tours Wednesday–Sunday 11am–5pm; Tel: 227-3956), the first house that Bulfinch designed for prominent lawyer, member of Congress, third Mayor of Boston, and developer of Beacon Hill, Mr. Otis. The 19th-century furnishings are opulent and surprisingly brilliantly colored.

The Esplanade

Explore westwards from Charles Street, and you'll come to the Esplanade, a long narrow park along the Charles River. Here Bostonians enjoy jogging, walking, cycling, in-line skating, or just watching the river life. The much-loved **Boston Pops Orchestra** performs in the Art Deco Hatch Memorial Shell during July; the 4th of July performance is a knockout (see page 84).

ALONG THE DOWNTOWN FREEDOM TRAIL TO DOWNTOWN CROSSING

From Brimstone Corner to Filene's

This area bordering the eastern side of the common is filled with historical imprints and some of the city's major architectural highlights, which are great when viewed from the harbor (see page 43).

Follow the Red Brick Line

The 3-mile (1½ km) **Freedom Trail** is a walking tour marked with a clear red line, which covers 16 historic buildings, sites and monuments that outline Boston's contribution to American history. Maps and brochures are available at the Boston Common Visitor Kiosk (Tel: 536-5100) at 147 Tremont Street.

Although it's only supposed to be 2.5 miles (4km) long, with all the twists and turns, it feels longer. Plan to spend at least four hours on the trail, or for an abbreviated tour, try stopping at the following: the Granary Burial Ground, Old South Meeting House, Faneuil Hall, Paul Revere House (Tel: 523-2338), Old North Church (Tel: 523-4848), U.S.S. Constitution (Tel: 242-5670), and Bunker Hill Monument. National Historic Park manages the trail: see page 109 for more details of tours.

Park Street Church stands on a site whose nickname comes from Brimstone Corner (some say for the fiery sermons delivered by such figures as Henry Ward Beecher and William Lloyd Garrison, who delivered his first anti-slavery speech here in 1829, others because gunpowder was kept in the basement during the 1812 War). Built on the site of a granary in 1809, this Georgian church's most beautiful feature is the 217-ft- (66-m-) tall triple-tiered steeple, based on a Christopher Wren design.

Erected in 1809, the Park Street Church stands proud on "Brimstone Corner."

The adjacent **Granary Burying Ground** contains the graves of many heroes: John Hancock, Paul Revere, Samuel Adams, James Otis, the victims of the Boston Massacre, Robert Treat Paine (the prosecutor at the Boston Massacre trial), and Peter Faneuil. A map near the entrance locates the gravestones of the famous. Note the many headstones carved with skull and crossbones or winged death's head motifs. Over the years headstones have been moved to accommodate newcomers and the lawnmower, so they may not mark accurately where the remains lie; furthermore, a couple of dozen bodies may be interred under each stone given that 2,300 bodies are buried here.

Continue northward along Tremont Street to the squat, granite **King's Chapel** (Tel: 227-2155). The first Anglican place of worship in Boston, it stands on land taken by Governor Andros from the burial ground next door: The Puritans refused to sell any land that would be used to benefit a denomination that had persecuted them. Royal officials and wealthy merchants worshiped here until the Revolution caused a split in the congregation and placed the church in jeopardy. After the Revolution it became the first Unitarian church in the nation, even while it retained much of the ritual and musical tradition of the earlier church (frequent lunchtime and other concerts are given).

The magnificent interior, one of the finest examples of Georgian church architecture in North America, has lavishly upholstered pews — especially the governor's — gilt crown and miters on the organ case, the oldest pulpit in the nation, and a bell cast by Paul Revere that was tolled at the time of his death.

Adjacent **King's Chapel Burial Ground,** is the city's oldest and holds many historical characters: first governor, John Winthrop; William Dawes, who rode with Paul Revere; and Elizabeth Pain, the model for Hawthorne's Hester Prynne in *The Scarlet Letter.* Charles Bulfinch is buried under the Chapel itself.

Follow the Freedom Trail to the Old State House for a look at colonial history.

Turn down School Street, to the mosaic plaque outside Old City Hall commemorating Boston Public Latin School, which was founded in 1635, the oldest school in the US. Benjamin Franklin was an early pupil, and his statue stands in the courtyard here. (Boston Latin is now situated in the Fenway; students there still have to study Latin.) The Beaux Arts City Hall has been replaced by nearby Government Center. It is now home to the Maison Henri, a highly recommended and popular French restaurant.

Back on the corner of Tremont Street, the Omni Parker House hotel (the oldest continually operating hotel in the nation) has been associated with much of the city's political and social history since it opened in 1854. John F. Kennedy announced his candidacy in the Press Room and to this day the bar is still a quintessential politician's bar. The Literary Club and Magazine Club met here gathering such figures as Richard Henry Dana, John Greenleaf Whittier, James Russell Lowell, and others. The *Atlantic Monthly* was founded here in 1857. Here too, Ho Chi Minh worked in the kitchens around 1915 and Malcolm X, who was born in Roxbury, worked as a busboy in the 1940s.

At School and Washington streets, the lovely red-brick building with a Dutch gambrel roof was built in 1718 as an apothecary shop on the site of Anne Hutchinson's residence. In the 19th century it became a literary light when Ticknor and Fields, the publisher of Emerson, Longfellow, and Thoreau operated here from 1832 to 1865 and when the *Atlantic Monthly* was the most famous magazine of the day.

Today the **Globe Corner Bookstore** sells memorabilia and souvenirs associated with the *Boston Globe* and the city. Across the street stands a moving monument to the two million Irish immigrants who fled starvation and oppression crossing "the bowl of tears" to seek a better life in Boston.

Diagonally opposite, stands the **Old South Meeting House** (1729). Here on 16 December, 1773, 5,000 colonists came to protest the tea tax. They listened to Samuel Adams and then marched down to the docks and dumped 123,000 pounds of tea into the harbor (see page 15). Ben Franklin was baptized here, and black poet Phyllis Wheatley worshiped here. During the occupation of Boston, the English desecrated the church ripping out the pews and using it as a riding school. Today it's been restored and visitors can enjoy an audio presentation about the great controversies that have been aired here.

Continue up Washington Street, into the heart of the Downtown shopping area (see page 80). Here the Freedom Trail doubles back on itself to the **Old State House** (1713), a red-brick building with a wedding cake bell tower. The surrounding buildings dwarf it. It was the British Government's headquarters in Boston and also served as the merchants' exchange and after the revolution as the state capitol. Here James Otis argued against the Writs of Assistance; the Declaration of Independence was read from the balcony on 18 July, 1776. The gold lion and silver unicorn above, symbols of the British crown, are replicas of originals that were destroyed that same day. Inside, displays and historical artifacts relate Boston's Revolutionary history. Other exhibits

The Basement

Not to be confused with Filene's, the department store upstairs, Filene's Basement (426 Washington Street, 9:30am–7:30pm, Monday–Friday; 9am–7:30pm Saturday; 11am–7pm Sunday) is the oldest discount store in the country selling stylish clothes from the mid-range to designer labels. Prices start low and can be marked down an additional 75 percent. You can't go wrong here.

concentrate on later events, like the first attempt to integrate the schools in 1848.

It's easy to miss the circle of stones in a traffic island in front of the Old State House marking the site of the **Boston Massacre.** Here on March 5, 1770, British soldiers, taunted by colonists, fired on an angry crowd, killing five, including Crispus Attucks, the first victim, who was black. The massacre aided the Revolutionary cause by creating its first martyrs and the propagandists, including Paul Revere, who made an engraving of the event, used it to their advantage.

The city's malls now outshine the shopping district of **Downtown Crossing** (around the crossroads of Washington, Summer, and Winter streets), but here you'll discover long-established department stores like Macy's and Filene's. It's hard to imagine the pedestrians-only Washington Street joining the Old State House south to the neck of the Shawmut peninsula before the landfills were created in the 19th century. A few quaint stores are hidden down side alleys, as is the 19th-century Locke-Ober (in Winter Place), which has served traditional fare to well-heeled businessmen for over a century.

GOVERNMENT CENTER & FANEUIL HALL

This is Boston's commercial and financial heart, but it's far from being an homogeneous district: It incorporates the austere Government Center and the lively Faneuil Hall Marketplace.

Government Center

Little good can be said about Government Center. It's monolithic, dreary, and soulless. The city has attempted to enliven the complex by adding a garden with terraces, pools, and niches where music is performed, but there's

With over 14 million visitors a year, Faneuil Hall boasts an assortment of shops and a historic galleried meeting hall.

still little reason to visit, except to see the enormous Steaming Kettle on the south side of the plaza above the door of the eponymous coffee shop. Commissioned by the Oriental Tea Company in 1873, it is an appropriate landmark for a city so closely linked to tea. Its capacity is printed on its side: 227 gallons, 2 quarts, 1 pint, 3 gills (some 868 liters).

Faneuil Hall Marketplace

Annually 14 million visitors come to **Faneuil Hall** (Tel: 242-5642), the great "Cradle of Liberty" and marketplace. It's very commercial, but very alluring and one of the most successful restorations anywhere.

Huguenot merchant Peter Faneuil (pronounced: *fan-yell* and *fan-nail*), gave it to the city in 1742. The original, consisting of a town hall above and a market below was burned down in 1762, but was swiftly rebuilt. Here on the second floor Boston's great orators raised their voices against British tyranny, against slavery, and female oppression. It's still used for meetings and assemblies. The vast painting behind the stage shows Daniel Webster and John Calhoun arguing over the Union. The building's most legendary feature is the grasshopper weathervane. No one knows really why tinsmith Shem Drowne chose the grasshopper motif, although some say it symbolizes good fortune. In 1805 Charles Bulfinch enlarged the hall.

Across the plaza from Fanueil Hall the three **Quincy market** buildings fill with crowds of locals and visitors, who come to feast on chowder, seafood, deli sandwiches, pizza, and an array of ethnic cuisines. They also come to shop at the stalls, the flower market, and the stores, to watch the street entertainers and to sample the nightlife. One restaurant in particular draws folks — **Durgin Park,** which offers Yankee cuisine, communal dining, and tough no-nonsense waitresses. When they were built in 1826, these buildings stood on the waterfront. Older Bostonians can still recall the stench of rancid meat emanating from them on a hot summer's day and the gradual decay of the area before they were restored in the late 1970s.

BLACKSTONE BLOCK AND THE NEW ENGLAND HOLOCAUST MEMORIAL

A neon sign northeast of the plaza, beckons visitors to the oldest restaurant in the United States, the **Ye Olde Union Oyster House** (see page 134) which opened in 1826 in the Blackstone Block, a tiny group of old red-brick buildings separated by narrow alleys that dates to 1713. Even if you don't intend to eat here, peer in the window at the oysters and clams being shucked at the raw bar (the establishment serves as many as 4,000 oysters on a busy day).

The Black Heritage Trail

Massachusetts declared slavery illegal in 1783. Boston had always had a substantial free black population but after 1783 it increased as many blacks settled in the North End and the north side of Beacon Hill. Free tours of the Black Heritage Trail are offered on weekdays at 10am, noon, and 2pm by reservation only. Tours begin at the Shaw Memorial. Call the Museum of Afro-American History (Tel: 739-0022) or the Boston African American National Historic Site (Tel: 742-5415) to make reservations 24 hours in advance. The memorial sculpted by St. Gaudens and erected in 1897, honors the first free black regiment and those who died in a famous Civil War battle. These black soldiers, whom St. Gaudens depicted individually with great care — revolutionary for the time — served without pay until granted a salary equal to their white counterparts. On the back of the memorial the white officers are praised for "casting their lot with men of a despised color." The tour's other focal point is the African Meeting House in Smith Court. The oldest black Baptist church in the US, it was formed in 1806, in response to discrimination at white churches. It became a major abolitionist center. William Lloyd Garrison founded the New England Anti-Slavery Society here in 1832. Upstairs in the meeting hall, Frederick Douglass spoke 40 times. Wendell Phillips and Charles Sumner also spoke to huge audiences. In the basement, the Museum of Afro-American History has a collection of historic pamphlets and works by contemporary black artists. At the corner of Smith Court and Joy Street, the nation's first black school, the Abiel Smith School is being restored.

Set back on a black granite path in front of the Blackstone block is the line of six luminous towers that constitute the **New England Holocaust Memorial**, which commemorates the six million Jews who died in Nazi death camps. Erected in 1985 by sculptor Stanley Saitowitz. Each of the 54-foot (16-meters) towers are lit internally to gleam at night, all baring the name of one of six major death camps – Auschwitz Birkenau, Chelmno, Sobibor, Treblinka, Majdanek and Belzec.

Don't miss the colorful fruit and vegetable market that takes place at the Haymarket, just behind Blackstone Block, on Friday and Saturday.

THE NORTH END AND ACROSS THE RIVER TO CHARLESTOWN

An Italian Festa

The North End with its Italian cafés and restaurants and vibrant street festivals is one of Boston's most entrancing neighborhoods. Before the Revolution, royal officials and other wealthy folk lived here, but in the 19th century it became a crowded slum as immigrants — Irish, Jewish, Portuguese, and Italian — poured into the district. Two retail titans got their start here on Hanover Street — Eben Jordan and R. H. Macy. "Honey Fitz," father of Rose Kennedy, was born on Ferry Street. The Italians took hold in the 1920s and made the area the lovable, close-knit community it is today, where ladies in aprons still feel free to loll outside in the evenings.

Hanover Street, is the North End's commercial backbone lined with cafés and restaurants frequented by locals from the community, not just tourists. On weekend evenings people gather for a liqueur and *gelati* at the cavernous Caffé Vittoria at number 296. Examine the walls for splendid black-and-white photographs of the area. **Salem Street,** just north of Hanover, is another atmospheric street lined with wonderful delicatessens redolent with the scents of fresh cheeses, sausages, and pasta, newsstands selling *Corriere della Sera* and *La Gazzetta dello Sport*, and such bakeries as Bova, selling first-rate cakes and pastries at number 134.

The Historical Sights

The clapboard **Paul Revere House,** tucked into pretty North Square, is the oldest building in downtown Boston, dating to 1680. Paul Revere purchased it in 1770 for £213, a sizable sum for an artisan. The exterior is notable for its diamond pane windows, deep second-story overhang, and massive chimneys. Inside, it's furnished with 17th-century pieces, but only a few letters and engravings recall Revere's life here.

Boat builder Nathaniel Hichborn, Revere's cousin, lived in what is now the **Pierce-Hichborn House,** one of the city's earliest brick Georgians built in 1711. On most days, there are two guided tours (details available from the Paul Revere House; Tel. 523-2338 for more information).

Back on Hanover Street, **St. Stephen's Church (1804)**, is Boston's only remaining Bulfinch church. It began as a

Built in 1804, St. Stephen's Church is the city's only Bulfinch church.

Congregationalist Church but since 1862 has served the Roman Catholic Irish, Italian, and Portuguese communities. John F. Fitzgerald, father of Rose Kennedy, baptized his daughter here. The church looks down what the locals call the Prado, officially named **Paul Revere Mall.** The equestrian statue of Paul Revere, set against the steeple of Old North Church rising out of the foliage, is one of the most photographed sights in the city. Locals chat on the stone benches of the promenade, while tourists inspect the bronze plaques on the brick walls that pay tribute to the North End's famous sons.

Old North Church (properly known as Christ Church) is the city's most beloved. Here on the night of 18 April, 1775, sexton Robert Newman climbed the tower and hung the two lanterns ("one, if by land, and two, if by sea") warning the colonists in Concord of British troop movements. The lanterns are lit on the eve of Patriot's Day each year (see page 91). Modeled on Christopher Wren's designs it was built in 1723. The steeple was added in 1740 and has toppled several times. The interior contains enclosed pews with brass nameplates of the original families who worshiped here, including the Reveres. Numerous memorials around the walls recall soldiers who died in the Revolution or Tories who fled the city.

The last Freedom Trail stop in the North End is **Copp's Hill Burying Ground,** which has a fine view across the river to Charlestown. Sexton Robert Newman, preacher Cotton Mather, and Prince Hall, a free black who founded the Negro Freemasons, are all buried here. Note too the pockmarks on some of the headstones caused by the British who used them for target practice before the Battle of Bunker Hill (see page 16).

Head west down Commercial and Causeway streets, and you will soon reach North Station and the site of the old **Boston**

Garden, the beloved arena for the Bruins ice hockey and the Celtics basketball teams until 1995. FleetCenter (Tel. 624-1000 for information on events) has now replaced it.

Charlestown

Across the river, the Charlestown Navy Yard has played a major role in Boston's history for nearly two hundred years. Today it's home to the indomitable "Old Ironsides," or the *U.S.S. Constitution,* a war ship that was built in 1797 in the North End for $302,718. During her naval career, she won 42 battles, captured 20 vessels, and was undefeated. Her most notable triumphs occurred during the War of 1812 when she vanquished the British ships *Guerriere*, *Java*, *Cyane*, and *Levant*. A British sailor gave her the name "Old Ironsides," as cannon balls skimmed off her copper sheathed gunwales and he marveled at her apparent indestructibility.

Today you can go aboard to see the decks. Every July 4th she fires a salute and is taken out on a short cruise. You can also visit

Italian *feste*

Most summer weekends, somewhere in the North End the neighborhood is celebrating in true Sicilian or Tuscan style. Usually they are celebrating a saint's day associated with their ancestral villages, back in Italy. Tinsel and lights are strung across the street and in the evenings a traditional brass band plays favorite melodies. Matronly Italian women sell raffle tickets and pin the proceeds on drapes hanging from the saint's statue, while kids toss basketballs and throw darts at fairground stalls. Other stalls sell calzones, mozzarella sticks, homemade meatballs, and fried calamari. Sunday is the day of the big procession, when the statue is carried aloft on the shoulders of neighborhood men while bystanders throw confetti and balloons.

the World War II destroyer ***U.S.S. Cassin Young*** and take guided tours of the Naval Yard conducted by the park rangers. At the adjacent **Constitution Museum** (Tel: 426-1812) you can computer skipper the *Constitution* through some of her famous battles and trace the route she took on her round the world trade mission in 1844. Exhibits also show how horrendous were the living conditions endured by her crew of 450.

American Colonel Prescott is immortalized at the base of the Bunker Hill Monument.

Nearby, the 220-ft- (67-m-) tall tapering granite obelisk, the **Bunker Hill Monument** (Tel: 242-5641) commemorates the first battle of the Revolution, on 17 June, 1775 — a hollow victory for the British who suffered more than 1,000 casualties against 400 to 600 for the colonials. Despite the name it actually stands on Breed's Hill, the site of the colonial redoubt in the battle.

At its base is a swashbuckling statue by William Wetmore Storey of American Colonel Prescott, who gave the famous order: "Don't fire 'til you see the whites of their eyes." There are informative models depicting the battle's progress as well as hourly musket-firing demonstrations. You can climb the 294 spiral steps to an enclosed deck, which has great views. A multimedia presentation at The Bunker Hill Pavilion re-enacts the battle.

To reach Charlestown: walk along the Freedom Trail (roughly a 15-minute walk from Copp's Hill to the Naval Yard) or take the Orange Line to Community College (10 minutes to Bunker Hill Monument), or else take the water shuttle from Long Wharf.

THE FINANCIAL DISTRICT & CHINATOWN

State Street originally linked the wharves to the Old State House. Today it is a commercial street boasting the showy glass tower of the Stock Exchange Building (53 Exchange Place), which features a monumental marble staircase in the foyer. Another ostentatious marble atrium foyer marks number 75. At the harbor end stands the bizarre **Custom House Tower,** a skyscraper that was added to a 19th-century Greek Revival temple base in 1913.

For a good look at Downtown's architecture, go to the green triangle of Post Office Square. Stepped sides and Art Deco–style wall decorations make the **New England Telephone Building** on the southern edge of the square one of the most arresting. The lobby's 360-degree mural celebrates the proletarian history of the telephone. You can also pop in to a little room off the

The Custom House Tower, overlooking State Street, dates back to 1913.

Boston Highlights

If you have limited time these are the must-see sights.

Back Bay: some of the finest Victorian residential architecture in the nation lines the broad avenues of this great enclave that includes shopping on Newbury Street. (See pages 47–50)

Beacon Hill: the city's most historic and picturesque neighborhood. (See pages 24–25)

Boston Museum of Science: an outstanding example of the genre.

Boston Pops: popular fun concerts by the Boston Symphony — in May, June, and on 4 July. (See page 84)

Cambridge: arguably America's most famous center of academia. (See pages 57–66)

Faneuil Hall Marketplace: one of Boston's most popular attractions, a touristy but fun mall. (See pages 32–33)

Filene's Basement: lowest prices in the famous bargain store. (See page 30)

The Freedom Trail: a trail marked by a red line connecting the city's famous historic monuments that recall the struggle for American Independence. (See page 26)

Isabella Stewart Gardner Museum: a wonderful personal collection displayed in a marvelous Venetian-style palazzo.

John F. Kennedy Library and Museum: a celebration of this President's 1000-day administration housed in a dramatic bayfront building by I. M Pei.

Skywalk Observatory: Located on the 50th floor of the Prudential Center

Museum of Fine Arts: a superb collection of European and American art, plus strong Japanese and Asian collections

New England Aquarium: a terrific example of the genre.

The North End: the lively Italian neighborhood.(See pages 35–38)

Public Garden: Boston's bosky garden. (See page 22)

The Red Sox: a must for baseball aficionados. (See pages 54 and 87)

Whale watching: Boston's biggest thrill. (See pages 46)

lobby that replicates the attic room of Alexander Bell on nearby Court Street. It was from there that he first transmitted sounds electrically over a wire in 1875 (open Monday–Friday, 8:30am–5pm).

There are said to be over 50 restaurants in **Chinatown,** the crowded blocks bordered by Washington, Kneeland, and Essex streets and the Expressway. Even if you don't intend to eat here, you might enjoy visiting some of the Chinese jewelry stores, groceries, and bakeries, on the streets that feature pagoda-topped telephone boxes. It's small compared to New York or San Francisco's sprawling Chinatowns, so don't bother unless you're really interested.

With over 100 sea-life species — fish, sharks, sea turtles, and more — the New England Aquarium is a must see!

THE WATERFRONT AND FORT POINT CHANNEL

Wharves reach out into Boston Harbor from Downtown and the North End like the fingers on a hand. Once this was the second busiest port in the United States, with clippers jostling for space. Today after a long period of decline, the area has revived and the granite warehouses have been renovated into apartments, restaurants, offices, and hotels. The British sailed home from **Long Wharf.** Today you can sail to the Harbor Islands, take a cruise around the harbor, or just sit and admire the craft at anchor.

On Central Wharf, the **New England Aquarium** is one of the best anywhere. Its centerpiece is a giant 200,000-gallon tank containing a 24-ft- (7-m-) deep coral reef filled with sharks, sea turtles, and 600 fish from 100 species. Five times a day, scuba divers go in to feed the fish, a fascinating spectacle to watch. Ramps circle the tank so that you can walk around the whole thing. More than 70 exhibit tanks make up the Aquarium galleries. They are categorized as salt or fresh water and feature communities of fish inhabiting different marine climates, from cold and temperate to tropical. Visitors can see the life forms found in a salt marsh, a mangrove swamp, or along the New England seashore. Kids love the Touch Tide Pool where they can handle crabs and starfish. Other perennial favorites are the penguins, the sea otters, and the sea lions, who provide entertainment in the theater. The aquarium is currently undergoing an expansion that will triple its size. The new West Wing containing a large outdoor seal exhibit, two floors of exhibits, plus visitor facilities opened in 1998. A large-format theater will open in 2001 and the new East Wing in 2003.

Tea overboard! Re-enact the famous event at the Boston Tea Party Ship and Museum.

To the south **Rowes Wharf** hosts many different cruise ships and also anchors the luxurious Boston Harbor Hotel.

Fort Point Channel divides Downtown from South Boston (confusingly to the east) and here, docked by one of the rusty bridges across the channel, *Beaver II* looks anachronistic. In a way it is, for it's a replica of one of the three ships that the Patriots, dressed as Indians, boarded and from which they dumped 342 chests of tea. Built in 1973 in Denmark it sailed across the Atlantic for the Bicentennial. On a short wharf in the Channel at Congress Street Bridge, stands the Boston Tea Party Ship and Museum, which consists of a small museum and the replica Beaver II, moored beside the museum.

Sadly, a fire in August of 2001 forced the closing of the museum, and at the time of writing there is no indication if or when it may reopen. Visitors may telephone 338-1773 for updates and information.

A superb museum for children stands across Fort Point Channel marked by a whimsical giant milk bottle, which serves snacks and ice cream. The **Children's Museum** is both a vast playground and a stimulating learning center. The buzz words here are "hands on": There are strange sculptures to climb over, bubbles to make, and hopscotch to play in Chinese and Italian in the Kid's Bridge — a reference to Boston's multiculturalism. The most original part of the museum is an entire Japanese house, with bathroom, kitchen, and tatami rooms, which have authentic scents, and Teen and Teen Tokyo, where you can ride the subway and take up the Sumo Challenge.

Cruises and Looking For Leviathans

On a fine day, a boat trip in Boston Harbor is idyllic. The rectangular, circular, and pyramidal shapes of the downtown rooflines are etched magnificently against the skyline. The water is bobbing with yachts, speedboats, tugs, and fishing craft, while a constant stream of jets descends onto the waterside runways of one of the world's busiest airports.

As you reach the outer harbor, the urban scenery fades, and a jumble of indecipherable green lumps appear. These are the 30 tiny islands that constitute **The Harbor Islands.** Gulls hover over lobster pots or perch on rocky outcrops; channel markers float on the surface and small lighthouses appear on the horizon.

There's not that much to do or see on the seven islands that make up Boston Harbor Islands State Park, but an afternoon spent here offers gentle strolls, picnics, and bird-watching — a welcome respite from urban frenzy. From May to mid-October, the Boston Harbor Cruise Company (Tel. 723-7800) operates a ferry from Long Wharf to **Georges Island,** the core of the group. Fort Warren, a 19th-century star-shaped fortress in which Confederate prisoners were incarcerated during the Civil War occupies most of the island. It's an atmospheric and spooky place, with old gun emplacements, lookout posts, and chilly alleys.

You can also visit five other islands — Peddocks, Lovells, Bumpkin, Gallops, and Grape — on a free water-shuttle service from Georges Island from July to Labor Day. Lovells is the only island with a designated swimming area. For details on camping, see page 120.

One of the most exciting experiences you can have in Boston is **whale-watching.** From April through to October, literally dozens of sightseeing craft from Boston and other ports scattered along the New England coast head out to an area known as Stellwagen Bank, where whales stock up on plankton and fish before migrating to warmer Caribbean climes. If you sail from Gloucester and Provincetown, which are closer to the Bank, you will spend less time getting there and more time actually looking for whales. For details of sightseeing and whale-watching trips, see page 111.

Humpbacks are most commonly spotted, but you might also spy the larger fin whales (which measure up to 80-ft or 24-m in length — the second biggest species after blue whales) and swift, 30-ft (9-m) -long minkes. You're almost certain to glimpse a whale. In fact, on a good day you may see as many as 40. (You are more likely to see greater numbers if the weather is poor; take seasickness medicine before boarding.) When the guide — who is usually a well-qualified naturalist — makes a sighting, everyone rushes to one side of the boat, causing it to lurch suddenly. The boat heads off toward the telltale sign of the spume of water, and then suddenly, there it is: a silvery flank virtually underneath the boat. A flick of a tail or fluke, and it's gone. If you are very lucky, you may see a whale breaching, heaving its entire body out of the water. At times, it seems as if the whales themselves are doing the watching, when they approach the boats, swim underneath them, and stare up at the tourists.

BACK BAY AND THE FENWAY

In the middle of the 19th-century, Boston ended at Boston Common and Back Bay was just a polluted tidal flat. In 30 years, however, an immense landfill project transformed it into the city's most fashionable residential and commercial district to which the well-to-do moved from Beacon Hill and the South End.

In contrast to the tangled maze of lanes of the "old" city, Back Bay was meticulously planned in regimented lines inspired by the boulevards of Paris. The residential district North of Boylston Street contains some of the best Victorian architecture in the country.

Churches and Skyscrapers

From the Public Garden, Boylston Street leads into the commercial section of Back Bay. Follow it a short way to **Copley Square,** a popular summer focal point for concerts, and a place where kids splash in the fountain. Here a feast of contrasting buildings competes for your attention.

☛ Sleek, blue **John Hancock Tower,** New England's tallest building, rises on one side. Two sides are knife-edge thin, and from certain

Built in 1877, Trinity Church holds its own next to the John Hancock Tower.

vantage points it seems as if the building virtually disappears. When it was built in 1976 it was a disaster because the glass blew out, so every sheet had to be replaced. A model of the city in 1775 brings home just how much of the present land was under water at one time. Increased concerns about security following terrorist attacks in September 2001 forced the indefinite closing of the John Hancock Tower's rooftop. At present there are no plans to reopen the observation deck to the public. Visitors seeking a comparable aerial view of the city should visit the Prudential Center's Skywalk Observatory.

People feared that the tower would eclipse one of its neighbors, **Trinity Church,** but the beauty of Henry Hobson Richardson's masterpiece now reflected in the tower's glass, has only been enhanced. The church has been named by the AIA one of the nation's ten best buildings. In 1877 when it was consecrated, it cost $750,000. For that amount the commissioners purchased the great stained glass windows by John LaFarge, Edward Burne-Jones, and William Morris in addition to the building itself. The church has had some colorful preachers too from patriot Sam Parker to Phillips Brooks, author of *O Little Town of Bethlehem,* and a prodigious gourmet, who also loved the track, billiards, and fly-fishing. Ironically, the

The Boston Public Library — the oldest free municipal library in the world.

Hancock tower enriched the church when the church won $11.6 million in a suit against its developers for damage caused during construction.

On the other side of the square the **Boston Public Library** (1895), the oldest free municipal library in the world), is well worth visiting. The grand Italian Renaissance building has several decorative highlights — the bronze doors by Daniel Chester French at the Dartmouth entrance, the double marble staircase graced with murals by Puvis de Chavannes and Edwin Austin Abbey, and on the third floor, by John Singer Sargent. The Johnson Building was added in 1972 and now the library holds more than six million books stored on 65 miles of shelves.

Copley Place, on Huntington Avenue, is a large shopping mall, anchored by two 1,000-room hotels, with a hundred-plus shops. A walkway connects it to the graceless 52-story **Prudential Center,** from which the famous amphibious vehicles leave on **Boston Duck Tours.** After touring the shops, go up to the Top of The Hub bar-restaurant and **Skywalk Observatory** on the 50th floor, which affords spectacular 360-degree views of Boston.

A little farther along Huntington Avenue, the **Christian Science World Headquarters** may not sound enticing (and indeed, the austerity of the administration buildings around a vast reflecting pool makes a somber first impression). Still, the huge basilica of the First Church of Christ, Scientist, a huge Byzantine-style church enveloping the original Mother Church is an amazing edifice. It can hold 4,000; its tiered seating makes it more like a theater than a place of worship. The organ, which is the focal point of the space, contains 13,595 pipes covering nine octaves. Except for quotations on the walls from the New Testament and Christian Science founder, Mary Baker Eddy, there's no decoration. Some stained glass windows are found in the older church, which also contains founder Mary Baker Eddy's chair. She only addressed the congregation twice, as she wished to avoid any personal idolatry. A guided tour is highly recommended (you can only visit the original church by joining a tour).

The Christian Science publishing building, adjacent to the church, houses an interesting phenomenon, the **Mapparium,** a 30-ft (9m)-wide glass globe, made of 608 stained glass panels that are lit from outside by 300 lights. You can stand on the bridge in the middle of the sphere and study this dramatic object created by Chester Lindsay Churchill between 1932 and 1935 (it shows the national borders as they were then).

A bird's-eye view of sprawling Commonwealth Avenue from atop the Prudential Tower.

The Chic and the Victorian

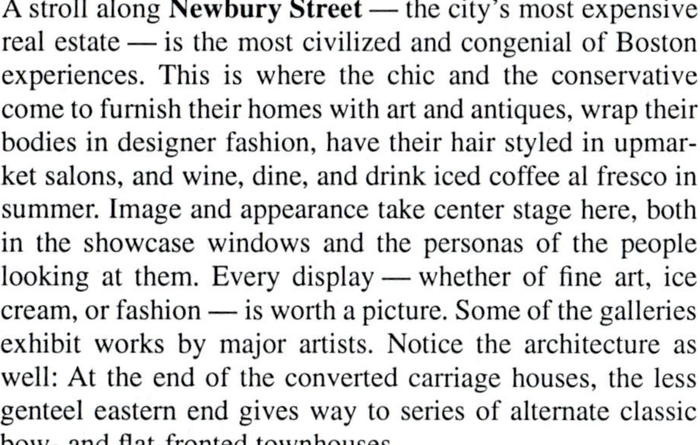

A stroll along **Newbury Street** — the city's most expensive real estate — is the most civilized and congenial of Boston experiences. This is where the chic and the conservative come to furnish their homes with art and antiques, wrap their bodies in designer fashion, have their hair styled in upmarket salons, and wine, dine, and drink iced coffee al fresco in summer. Image and appearance take center stage here, both in the showcase windows and the personas of the people looking at them. Every display — whether of fine art, ice cream, or fashion — is worth a picture. Some of the galleries exhibit works by major artists. Notice the architecture as well: At the end of the converted carriage houses, the less genteel eastern end gives way to series of alternate classic bow- and flat-fronted townhouses.

Take a detour along the way down one of the side streets, alphabetically arranged from A to H, starting at the Public Garden (they're named after English peers). In between the avenues, look out for the narrow, arrow-straight service alleys that form the entranceway to the old servants' quarters at the backs of the houses. The strip which is lined with elms and runs down the spine of **Commonwealth Avenue** is the perfect vantage point on which to stand back and gaze at the ornate Victorian buildings built in a range of styles — French Second Empire, Victorian Gothic, and Renaissance Revival. Detour to see the mansion designed by McKim Mead & White for John F. Andrew at 32 Hereford Street and to the building that housed the original Fannie Farmer Cooking School at 40 Hereford Street. You can get a wonderful sense of life in a Victorian Back Bay home at the **Gibson House,** at 137 Beacon Street, (open for tours May–October, Wednesday–Sunday at 1, 2, and 3pm, week-

ends the rest of the year). The contents of the house — imported carpets, plush Turkish ottomans — are the fascinating and colorful legacy of three generations of Gibsons, who lived here from 1860 to 1954.

Fenway

Come to Fenway to enjoy the city's two superb art museums, located close to the meandering tract of ponds, reeds, and meadows of the Back Bay Fens, and to see the Red Sox in action at **Fenway Park** (Tel: 267-9440 or 236-6666). Its center, Kenmore Square, pinpointed from afar by a massive neon CITGO sign, is a congested intersection of fast-food restaurants, frequented by local youth and university students from MIT and other colleges.

The **Museum of Fine Arts** (or MFA; Tel: 267-9300) contains one of the most important art collections in the country. There's much — too much — to absorb in one visit, so choose particular galleries or take a Highlights Tour leaflet and pick out just a few works. For example, the museum's outstanding collections of Asian works include Japanese armor, Javanese statue gods, Thai Buddhas, and Indian elephants. There are first-rate Egyptian galleries with mummies and early sculptures, and Nubian statues and stelae. The American galleries feature a full cupboard of silver made by Paul Revere, and his portrait (among many others) by John Singleton Copley, who was probably Boston's best-known artist. The complete pantheon of European art is represented — from the Italian Renaissance to English landscape painters.

The most overwhelming rooms are those exhibiting works by 19th-century French artists, containing dozens of Monets, Millet's *The Sower*, Renoir's *Dance at Bougival,* and works by Cézanne, Toulouse-Lautrec, and Van Gogh. There's also a great museum shop, a café, and a restaurant.

Nothing in Boston can match the beauty of the courtyard in the **Isabella Stewart Gardner Museum** (Tel: 566-1401). Modeled on a Venetian loggia, the cloister, delicate arches, and salmon-pink marble walls enclose a stunning, atmospheric space lined with mosaic and filled with foliage and classical statuary. Isabella Gardner created Fenway Court in 1903 to hold her outstanding collection of art. A flamboyant New Yorker, her unconventional ways scandalized the Boston Brahmins on more than one occasion. Her portrait by John Singer Sargent (in the Gothic Room) captures her individuality and her eccentricity lives on in her will, which stipulates that all of the 2,000 pieces on display in the house must be left exactly where they are. This decree is qualified by the condition that were anything to change, the museum's contents would be sold off, with the proceeds going to Harvard University.

It's an extraordinary place filled with great art works which are displayed idiosyncratically in often (for the time) innovative ways. It's more a personal home than a museum and the works are often poorly lit and cursorily labeled. Each of the museum's rooms display art of a particular artist — Titian, Raphael, or Veronese — or school — Dutch, Gothic, or early Italian.

Let's play ball! Catch a little Red Sox action at the bustling Fenway Park.

A Night Out with the Red Sox

Leave the car behind and experience being crushed by fans in a trolley on the MBTA Green Line to Kenmore. Constructed in 1912, Fenway Park is the oldest ballpark in the country. The quirky, irregularly shaped arena boasts real, manicured grass and a towering wall that is nicknamed the Green Monster for its scale and color. This is an intimate place, so even those who are standing at the back will be close to the action. If you're not familiar with baseball's finer points, most fans in the friendly, vociferous, 34,000-strong crowd would love to talk you through them. In a low-scoring game dominated by the pitchers, you might wonder what the fuss is about. Feel the fever generated by a slick double play or a home run, and you could be hooked. For tickets, see page 119.

BAY VILLAGE & THE SOUTH END

The few blocks of tiny **Bay Village** lie well hidden in between the Theater District and Back Bay, around Winchester, Melrose, and Fayette streets. It feels somewhat like a toy village — a miniature, flat version of Beacon Hill — with similar red-brick and black-shuttered homes lining sidewalks that are shaded by trees and lit by old-fashioned street lamps. These were the homes of artisans, not Brahmins, and are less precious, devoid of cornices and fancy wrought iron. When the marsh of Back Bay was filled in during the 1860s, water flooded into this area, forcing the streets and houses to be raised on pilings.

Take Tremont Street south and cross over the Massachusetts Turnpike into the **South End.** Come if only to savor one (or more) of its great restaurants, a clutch of chic bistros on Tremont Street around Clarendon. Like so much of Boston, the South End began as a landfill project, but it soon lost out in desirability to Back Bay. A multi-ethnic mix of Hispanic, Irish, West Indian, and Greek, the community is also home to Boston's largest gay community. Some districts — to the south of Shawmut Avenue, for example — are best avoided. In others, though, you will come across bright community murals and perhaps a reggae band playing in a local park.

The neighborhood boasts (justifiably) a fine concentration of Victorian terraced residences. Bow brick houses, their steep stoops (or steps) framed with scrolled black railings, are set off by parks, the finest examples being Union Park Square, situated just off Tremont Street, and Rutland and Concord squares both farther to the south.

SOUTH BOSTON, DORCHESTER, & JAMAICA PLAIN

Although the Boston suburbs might not claim any "must see" sights, if you have a car and are confident about finding your way around with a good map, there is a variety of intriguing places to explore.

South Boston, referred to as Southie, is in fact (rather confusingly) situated east of Downtown. Home to such establishments as Flanagan's Supermarket and the Shannon Tavern on its main thoroughfare of East Broadway, it's thoroughly and proudly Irish. In fact, it was the flashpoint for protests and riots during the busing controversy in the 1970s. Follow the main street past its old wooden and brick houses down to **Fort Independence,** which stands at the very mouth of Boston Inner Harbor. The fort is rarely open, but join the locals who settle down in the surrounding park with deck chairs and binoculars to watch the nautical and aeronautical activity. Your next stop could well be **Dorchester Heights,** a three-tiered tower of marble standing on a hill.

From here in 1776 George Washington trained his artillery on the city and succeeded in frightening British troops into evacuating Boston. (see page 16).

Follow the waterfront south to the extraordinary, stark white building designed by I. M. Pei for the **John F. Kennedy Library and Museum** (Tel: 929-4500). Enter via the brilliantly lit atrium with glorious bayfront view. See the introductory film and then look at the 25 exhibits that trace the career of John F. Kennedy using rare film and television footage, documents, and personal memorabilia. You can watch the Kennedy/Nixon debate again, revisit the 67-day 1960 campaign and see Walter Cronkite reading the results. Other exhibits highlight the accomplishments of the 1,000 days — the resolution of the Cuban Missile Crisis, the founding of the Peace Corp, the launching of the space program, and the support for Civil Rights. The film footage of the assassination still shocks and appalls. The quotation that follows "A man may die, nations may rise and fall, but an idea lives on" though reminds us of an earlier political time when visionary ideas mattered more than gossip to the media commentators (see page 111 for details of boat trips from Downtown). **Franklin Park and Zoo** (Park Tel. 635-7383, Zoo Tel. 541-5466), a

Boston Common — the historical and geographical heart of the city.

75-acre (30-hectare) area with 150 different species, is part of the park. The showpieces are the new lion exhibit, snow leopard and cheetah exhibits, and an African tropical rain forest, which is complete with gorillas and warthogs. Franklin Park was the jewel in the **Emerald Necklace,** the last in a 7-mile (11-km) network of parks designed by Frederick Law Olmsted that run all the way from Boston Common.

West of Franklin Park, lies the 265-acre (107-hectare) **Arnold Arboretum** (Open dawn-dusk daily. Admission free. Visitors' Center open May–October 9am–4pm Monday –Friday; November–April 10am–2pm Saturday and Sunday). Each of the 15,000 trees, shrubs, and vines, is labeled clearly with its common and scientific name. Spring is a good time to visit when the lilacs, rhododendron, and magnolia are in bloom; the 130 different maples put on a blazing show in the fall. Before returning to Boston, make a stop in affluent town of Brookline, once home to Olmsted. The modest wooden house at 83 Beals Street (a National Park Service property, open 10am–4:30pm, mid-May–October) is the **John F. Kennedy National Historic Site.** He was born and lived here until age four. His mother, Rose, had it restored with family pieces.

CAMBRIDGE

Cambridge is a distinct city with a distinct outlook. It's dominated by two of America's leading academic establishments, Harvard and MIT, and although there is a community outside the universities, visitors should begin by exploring life around Harvard Square.

Harvard Square and Harvard University

Harvard Square itself is unkempt. What makes it special is the people. This is a place where everyone just hangs out,

The Harry Widener Library, named after a victim of the ill-fated Titanic, is the largest university library in the world.

from students conversing in sententious tones, to punks in leather, and professionals in well-pressed suits. Street performers — fire jugglers, puppeteers, trapeze artists, musicians (Joni Mitchell and Tracy Chapman both performed here) — pull big crowds, notably on weekend evenings.

There are numerous cafés and bookshops (see page 61) in which to while away several hours. Buy a newspaper from the global selection at Out of Town News in the center of the square itself (the name also refers to all the surrounding streets), and settle down at Au Bon Pain café. It's *the* place for people-watching, and for a couple of dollars you can also test your skills against the resident chess maestro.

Among American universities, Harvard University is the oldest (founded in 1636 as a training ground for puritan ministers), and the richest, and has produced numerous Nobel Prize winners.

From Harvard Square enter the gates into **Harvard Yard,** the oldest part of the university. Here is Hollis Hall attended by Emerson and Thoreau, Massachusetts Hall attended by John and Samuel Adams, H. H. Richardson's Sever Hall, and Charles Bulfinch's Stoughton and University Halls. Note the statue of John Harvard, labeled as the founder and dated 1638. It's called the statue of the Three Lies because it isn't John Harvard, but only a student model; he wasn't the founder, only the first benefactor, who donated his 400-book library; and the date is wrong (it should be 1636). So much for Harvard's motto: *Veritas*, the Latin for "Truth."

In the second quad, the colossal pillars of the **Widener Library** face across the green to the Memorial Church, which has an elegant white spire peeping out above the foliage. The Widener houses about a third of the University's collection of 13 million volumes making it the largest university library in the world. It's named after Harry Elkins Widener, who drowned on the *Titanic* because he couldn't swim 50 yards to the lifeboats. His mother funded the establishment of the library, on condition that every Harvard graduate be able to swim 50 yards. Go in to view the John Singer Sargent's murals, Harry's book collection, including a 1623 Shakespeare portfolio and a Gutenberg Bible from 1450, and whatever is being shown in the Houghton Library.

Other notable buildings on campus include the **Carpenter Center for the Visual Arts,** the only building by Corbusier in North America (on Quincy Street), and the **Harkness Commons and Graduate Center** by Walter Gropius near Oxford and Everett streets.

Art and Science

Harvard has several fine museums. The most enjoyable is the **Fogg** (Tel: 495-2397) on Quincy Street, just off the northeast corner of Harvard Yard. The collection has some truly fine early Italian Renaissance paintings, which are displayed in the 16th-century Italian-style loggia modeled on a canon house in Montepulciano. The collection also contains some fine European and American paintings including works by Rembrandt, Dürer, Picasso, Chagall, and the Impressionists. See also the University's ceremonial silver and the Great Chair, a triangular-shaped affair, on which the incumbent Harvard president has to sit at the start of each year.

Connected to the Fogg the **Busch-Reisinger Museum** (Tel: 495-9400), displays a small but exquisite collection of German Expressionist works including Franz Marc's compelling *Horses*, and paintings by Kirchner, Klimt, Kandinsky, and Klee. Nearby the **Arthur M. Sackler Museum** occupies a dramatic, modern building designed by British architect James Stirling. It holds an important collection of classical and ancient works of art of Asian and Islamic origin. The ancient Chinese bronzes (some dating back to the 14th century B.C.) and the carved jades from the Shang Dynasty are particularly rewarding.

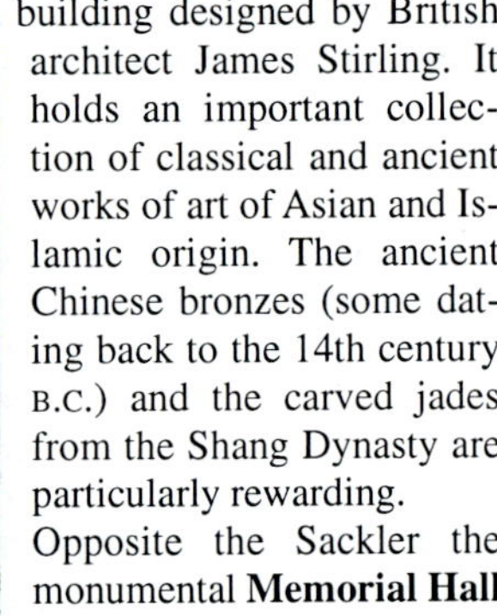

Opposite the Sackler the monumental **Memorial Hall** was in fact built to commemorate former students who

Find out why this Harvard Yard statue is nicknamed "The Statue of Three Lies."

died on the Union side in the Civil War. If it's open, peek inside the lovely wooden Sanders Theater and the reception hall.

A few steps north up Oxford Street or Divinity Avenue, the four **Harvard University Museums of Cultural and Natural History** are conveniently grouped together under one roof. Each merits a visit; allow several hours to do them justice. The best part of the Peabody Museum of Archeology and Ethnology Museum is the Hall of North American Indians, which focuses on ten different tribes, their particular lifestyles and how they are differentiated from each other.

Don't miss the meteorites in the Mineral and Geological Museums. In addition, the Botanical Museum has a world-

A Bibliophile's Paradise

Cambridge has more bookshops per capita than anywhere else in the US — more than 25 at the last count. Many specialize in topics — mystery, poetry, feminism, foreign literature, the occult — and most play a fundamental role in day-to-day life, acting not just as bookshops, but also as places to hang out and socialize. Many also stay open until 11pm seven nights a week.

Brattle Book Shop, 9 West Street, at Washington Street, Downtown – a treasure trove of antiquarian books._

Harvard Book Store 1256 Massachusetts Avenue, across from Harvard University, Cambridge. Selling new and used books focused largely on academic texts.

Grolier Poetry Bookshop, 6 Plympton Street, Harvard Square — a tiny, atmospheric haunt of overflowing shelves.

Waterstone's, 26 Exeter Street (at Newbury Street), Back Bay — a British shop; civilized and spacious.

WordsWorth Books, 30 Brattle Street, Harvard Square — stocks lots of discounted titles, good for bargain buys.

renowned collection of 3,000 glass flowers crafted in Germany between 1887 and 1936 for use in plant study. Each flower, plus all of its component parts — pistil, stamen, and so on — are replicated for 937 species. They are stunning works of art. Children enjoy the prehistoric fossils, the whale skeletons, and the menagerie of stuffed animals in the Museum of Comparative Zoology.

In and Around Brattle Street

Start down Brattle Street from Harvard Square. The Blacksmith House Bakery operates from the home of the blacksmith on whom Longfellow based "Under the spreading chestnut tree the village smithy stands" — although the tree is long gone. It is however memorialized in steel by artist-blacksmith Dimitri Gerakaris. Past the Loeb Drama Center, Brattle Street becomes more residential. H. H. Richardson designed Stoughton House at number 90. Many of the other mansions that line the street belonged to Loyalists, which is why the street was dubbed Tory Row in the 18th century.

One of these is the 28-room yellow clapboard **Longfellow National Historic Site**, which was commandeered by Washington as his headquarters during the siege of Boston (see page 16). Henry Wadsworth Longfellow, one of America's best-loved poets lived here for 45 years while he served as a professor of modern languages at Harvard. Visitors can view his study and library and other memorabilia. Incidentally, the chair in his study was made with wood from the chestnut tree of *The Village Blacksmith* poem. Summer concerts and poetry readings are organized in the pretty garden Take the car or a bus west down Brattle Street to the beautiful Victorian **Mount Auburn Cemetery,** the first "garden cemetery" in the nation laid out in 1831. At the

Interior of the Longfellow House — home of the esteemed poet, and one-time headquarters for George Washington.

entrance, pick up a horticultural map that will help guide you through the acres of landscaped banks, ponds, and trees and a map locating the graves of the many famous people who are laid to rest here, including Longfellow, Mary Baker Eddy, and Isabella Gardner. It's beautiful in spring when the dogwood and azalea bloom.

Head back down Brattle Street past **Radcliffe Yard** on the left, an elegant octagon of buildings carefully set around lawns. Radcliffe was established in 1879 as a women-only college; in 1999 it formally merged with Harvard. Exit Radcliffe Yard to **Cambridge Common,** where Washington first inspected the troops on 3 July 1775 (the elm tree that supposedly marks the site is not the original). Follow Garden Street east to Anglican Christ Church, which during the Revolution was used as a barracks by the colonists. Next door the burial ground is called God's Acre; it is the resting-place of early Harvard presidents and Revolutionary soldiers.

If you have time explore some of the side streets off Massachusetts Avenue to the north, which are lined with gracious clapboard homes. If you're looking for an evening alternative to Harvard Square, head to Hispanic-flavored **Inman Square**, located down Cambridge Street.

KENDALL SQUARE & EAST CAMBRIDGE

The **Massachusetts Institute of Technology** (MIT), founded in 1861 is America's leading science and engineering establishment that has pioneered many modern technologies, from stroboscopic photography to food

Mind over matter — an aerial view of M.I.T., America's leading science and engineering establishment.

preservation processes. Its graduates have started 4,000 companies and the list of its Nobel Prize Winners is long. The modern campus which has 28,000 students feels and looks very different from Harvard. Secure a map at the Information Center (located in the Rogers Building, 77 Massachusetts Avenue) and take a self-guided tour or join one of the student-led tours that are given weekdays. The **MIT Museum's Strobe Alley** (77 Massachusetts Avenue, Building Four, fourth floor; Tel: 253-4629) and **MIT's Compton Gallery** (77 Massachusetts Avenue on the MIT Campus; Tel: 253-4444) explore the relationship between art, science, and technology.

The List Visual Arts Center (20 Ames Street, at Main Street, Cambridge; Tel: 253-4680) puts on challenging contemporary art exhibitions. To the west of the Rogers Building, see Eero Saarinen's striking, glass-sided Kresge Auditorium and circular, moated brick chapel. Other notable buildings include: Alvar Aalto's Baker House, I. M Pei's Weisner Building, Green, Dreyfus and Landau Buildings, and Eduardo Catalano's Stratton Student Center. MIT also has a superb sculpture collection containing works by Alexander Calder, Louise Nevelson, and Frank Stella. See the Henry Moore piece in Killian Court, east of the Rogers Building and Calder's *The Big Sail* outside the Dreyfus Building.

A shuttle bus runs between Kendall Square, at the eastern edge of the MIT campus, and the CambridgeSide Galleria. The impressive waterfront mall has a number of large department stores and many smaller specialty shops.

You could spend a whole day in the **Museum of Science** (Tel: 723-2500; www.mos.com) complex that straddles the Charles River, playing and learning on the 400-plus interactive exhibits. Some of these, such as those on mathematics and biotechnology would stimulate an MIT graduate, while many others appeal to young children. Highlights include: the electron microscope that magnifies objects 25,000 times; a variety of dinosaur models and fossils; games that show how the human body works; stimulating games for learning about energy; and a rain forest re-creation. The demonstrations are thrilling too. Try to catch the world's biggest Van de Graaff generator going through its paces at the Theater of Electricity. In late 1999 The Museum of Science announced that it was merging with the old Computer Museum and so the museum now has a couple of interactive computer-oriented exhibits.

There are also laser and stargazing shows in the **Charles Hayden Planetarium**, and brilliant 3-D films shown in the Mugar Omni Theater. River trips offering good views of Back Bay leave from the Galleria and the Science Museum (see page 110). Nearby, on the downtown side of the river, the new temple of this sport- crazy town rises beside North Station. In 1995 FleetCenter replaced the old Boston Garden where fans had cheered on such legends as Bobby Orr of the Boston Bruins and Larry Bird of the Celtics. Tours are given of the new facility.

DAY TRIPS FROM BOSTON

If you only take one trip from Boston, make it to Lexington and Concord where the American Revolution began with a skirmish and the shot that was "heard around the world" was fired. The best way to reach both towns and to tour the sites is by car (half an hour or 14 miles/22 km west of Boston on Route 2 and Route 4/225). You can see the main historical sights in a day, but you'll need a second visit to appreciate Concord's rich literary heritage. During the summer and every year on Patriot's Day (see page 91), battles are staged, and the militiamen demonstrate their drill. Call (978) 369-3120 for further details.

Lexington

At **Lexington Battle Green** on 19 April, 1775 Captain Parker lined up 77 Minutemen (ready "at a minute's notice") against the 700 advancing British soldiers. His orders were: "Stand your ground! Don't fire unless fired upon! But if they mean to have a war, let it begin here." The Redcoats fired killing eight colonists.

The Hayes Memorial — in memory of those who fought in the Revolutionary War.

A plaque marks the triangular green as the "Birthplace of American liberty" and a burial monument honors "The first victims to the sword of British tyranny and oppression." A defiant Minuteman peers along the main street in the direction from which the Redcoats came. Visitors can see the interiors of three significant buildings associated with the battle: the **Buckman Tavern,** where the Minutemen gathered before the British arrival; the **Munroe Tavern** (Tel: 1-781-862-1703), the British Headquarters and field hospital; and the **Hancock-Clark House** (Tel: 1-781-862-1703), in which John Hancock and Samuel Adams were sleeping when Paul Revere arrived.

Concord

Route 2A links Lexington and Concord running through the 750-acre (303-hectare) National Historic Park. Stop first at the Battle Road Visitor Center. Here along this road, on the afternoon of 19 April 1775, the patriots harried the retreating British. Today, you can stop at the Paul Revere Capture site and Hartwell Tavern, a typical country inn.

In Concord, head to **Old North Bridge,** at the western end of the park to visit the spot where "the embattled farmers stood by the rude bridge and fired the shot heard 'round the world." It's bucolic today, but here the colonists clashed again with the British and killed 200 Redcoats. Cross the rickety bridge (not the original) to view the Minuteman Statue, equipped with rifle and plough. Follow the path up to the Visitor Center at the top of the hill, where you can watch a video about the battle and buy a Bill of Rights souvenir.

Concord's literary heritage is rich indeed, for it was the cradle of Transcendentalism and the place where Nathaniel Hawthorne, Ralph Waldo Emerson, Louisa May Alcott, and Henry David Thoreau all wrote. Today, you can visit four buildings associated with their movement.

The **Old Manse** (Tel: 1-978-369-3909)is beautifully situ-

All hands on deck! Explore the "Mayflower II," an exact replica of the original ship.

ated in a field next door to North Bridge. Reverend William Emerson, who built it, watched the battle from the window; his grandson Ralph later lived here. On the outskirts of town, on or near Route 2A are: **Emerson House** (Tel: 1-978-369-2236), which is full of Ralph's memorabilia; the enchanting **Orchard House** (Tel: 1-978-369-4118), owned by the Alcotts (including Louisa, who wrote *Little Women* here), and the **Wayside,** which was home to both the Alcotts and Nathaniel Hawthorne. Concord is also synonymous with Thoreau. Pack a picnic and follow Walden Street and Route 126 to **Walden Pond** (Tel: 1-978-369-3254), a lake fringed with tiny sandy beaches and enclosed by dense woods (be warned: it can get very crowded). Here, Henry David Thoreau, philosopher, essayist, poet, and friend of Emerson, lived in a cabin from 1845 to 1847, and wrote *Walden.* Near the main parking lot is a replica of his hut, containing a bed, table, desk, three chairs, and a stove.

Plymouth

Less than an hour from Boston, Plymouth doesn't let you forget its famous heritage, but unless you really want to see the rock that marks where the pilgrims landed in 1620 you might prefer to head on to Cape Cod. In Plymouth see ***Mayflower II*,** a replica of the original that was built in England, and sailed across the Atlantic in 1957. It gives you a good idea of just how cramped it was for the original 102 passengers on their 66-day voyage. Wander the decks and talk to the actors who play the parts of sailors and pilgrims. Nearby **Plymouth Rock** is not much to look at, but it is regarded as a national symbol of civil and religious freedom. Two miles south of town, **Plimouth Plantation** (Tel: 508-746-1622) shows life as it was in 1627. The "villagers" reside in wattle and daub huts, and chatter away about their religious beliefs and lifestyles as they tend their cows, sheep, and pigs. Nearby Hobbamock, a Native American neighbor, lives at his campsite. The entrance fee is high, but for those who appreciate these kinds of re-creations it's worth it. Note that you can buy a discounted combination ticket covering both the plantation and *Mayflower II.*

Back in town, the **Pilgrim Hall Museum** displays possessions of the Pilgrims, such as bibles and a cradle, and the original compacts from King James I to the settlers. Whale watches also operate from the harbor.

Cape Cod

Fabulous beaches, dramatic dunes, fragile salt marshes, and brilliant light have long drawn people, particularly artists to Cape Cod, "the bare and bended arm of Massachusetts."

In summer, it is incredibly crowded, and so if you can, you should avoid the Friday evening mass exodus, (see page 105) and visit during the week or off-season when it's only an hour from Boston to Sandwich, the nearest town on the Cape. With so many alluring inns, however, why not plan to stay overnight, but make sure to reserve in advance. Provincetown is right at the end of the Cape and in summer can most easily be reached from Boston via the ferry operated by Bay State Cruise Company (Tel. 748-1428).

The most alluring section of the Cape is its north shore and "upper arm." Beaches vary. The sheltered Cape Cod Bay beaches on the north shore are transformed into mud flats when the tide is out. The spectacular East Coast Atlantic beaches can have a strong undertow. On a sunny summer's day parking lots at the latter fill up fast; at many beaches visitors need a parking permit, which can be obtained from the town hall.

After crossing the Sagamore Bridge turn on to **Route 6A** which travels from one village to another past stately clapboard homes, antique stores and galleries, and other

Provincetown Harbor — easily accessible via ferry for Bostonians and visitors alike in search of a coastal getaway.

appealing stores. Numerous side roads lead to the relaxing Bay beaches.

The first town **Sandwich,** is the Cape's oldest community. It has a couple of sites worth visiting — the Sandwich Glass Museum and the Heritage Plantation. The first displays the brilliantly colored glass that was manufactured here in the 19th century, the second is an estate owned by Charles Dexter where you can see a dazzling display of antique cars, bird carvings by Elmer Crowell, a beautifully restored carousel, and more. The gardens alone are worth visiting, especially in spring when the rhododendrons bloom.

Several of the sea captain's homes along **Brewster**'s main street have been turned into country inns. Today this is the Cape's richest community.

The easiest way to reach the dramatic **Cape Cod National Seashore** is via the high-speed ferry to **Provincetown.** Here

With an "anything goes" attitude, a variety of shops, and local art galleries, Provincetown doesn't miss a beat.

on the outer elbow facing the Atlantic Ocean you can listen to the pounding surf and stroll the awesome beaches that are backed by huge dunes. Because the dunes are so fragile, access is strictly controlled and limited to boardwalks at some points. The National Seashore has two Information Centers: The Salt Pond Center, near Eastham on Route 6, and Province Lands Visitor Center just outside P-town. Both provide detailed information on the terrain, natural life, and activities. Just outside Provincetown, at Province Lands, take the opportunity to climb on to the roof for a panoramic view of the dunes, tenuously anchored by pitch pines and oaks.

There's an even better view from the top of the 253-ft (77-m) Pilgrim Monument in **Provincetown.** It's called the Pilgrim monument because this is where the Pilgrims actually landed first before moving on to Plymouth. The museum at the base of the tower tells the story.

P-Town, is a fabled place. Although the main street is crowded and lined with commercial tourist trinket stores, it still has a magical atmosphere, because it has an "anything goes" attitude. It is the East Coast's gay mecca (along with the Hamptons, and Cherry Grove and the Pines on Fire Island). Same-sex couples walk the streets hand in hand, and outrageous transvestites entertain in the cabarets. Families come to browse the stores selling T-shirts, and scrimshaw and driftwood curios, and to enjoy the beaches and the fishing and whale-watch trips. In the early 20th century Provincetown was a major art colony and there are still numerous art galleries, particularly at the east end of town.

In summer, the town is swamped and every guesthouse filled. In winter, it's quiet. Many of the commercial stores close and only the residents remain — a community of artists, Portuguese fishermen, and a handful of restaurateurs. You can visit Provincetown for a day (see page 110), but if you don't stay longer, you'll miss half the fun.

For a less frenetic pace and picturesque harbor, visit **Wellfleet**, a few miles south. It has its own share of galleries and leftover beatniks, but is decidedly more laid back.

Salem and Marblehead

Past the ugly northern suburbs of Boston lies a lovely rocky coastline from Marblehead to Cape Ann, studded with picturesque harbors, fine sandy beaches, and the elegant homes of wealthy Bostonians.

Although commuter trains (see page 117) run from Boston to Salem, Manchester, Gloucester, and Rockport, in most cases you are discharged a long way from beaches and sights so again you really need a car. In summer, the traffic isn't quite as appalling as on Cape Cod, but that's not saying much.

From Boston, follow Route 1A then 129 to **Marblehead,** about 16 miles away. The first people to settle here were Cornish fishermen. Now you can hardly see the water for moored yachts; halyards clink and large cars are parked outside exclusive sailing clubs. The superb natural harbor is formed by Marblehead Neck, which has a tiny park at its tip. The Old Town, with its narrow, sloping streets and early 18th-century buildings, each marked with the date it was built and the names and occupations of the original owners, is worth exploring.

A Bewitching City

In **Salem** magic bookshops, fortune tellers, a witch house, dungeon, and museum all recall the town's witchcraft trials of 1692, but there is much more to this town than witches. Start at the National Park Visitors Center at Museum Place (on Essex Street), where you can pick up some literature and a map of the Heritage Trail. The outstanding **Peabody Essex Museum** (Tel: 1-800-745-4054), tells the story of the development of this wealthy seaport town, which produced America's first millionaire, Elias Hesketh Derby. Kids will love the **Salem Witch Museum** (Tel: 1-978-744-1692), a diorama show that tells the story of the witch hysteria when 19 people went to the gallows.

Kids always enjoy the diorama show featured at the Salem Witch Museum.

Go beyond these sights to Nathaniel Hawthorne's **House of the Seven Gables** (Tel: 1-978-744—0991). Hawthorne of course worked at the Custom House and was also born in one of the houses nearby. The Heritage trail will return you to the lovely, red-brick marketplace, where the trial of Bridget Bishop is re-enacted (with the audience judging her fate). Additional information about attractions can be found at the Salem National Visitors' Center (2 Liberty Street, Salem; open daily 9am-5pm; Tel: 1-978-740-1650).

Cape Ann

From Salem the coast road (Route 127) to Cape Ann goes through Manchester, which has the lovely, sandy Singing Beach. Just past Magnolia **Hammond Castle Museum** looms above the entrance to Gloucester Harbor. Inventor John Hays Hammond, Jr. built this medieval-style castle to house his early Roman, medieval, and Renaissance collections. It also contains an 8,200-pipe organ (concerts are given).

Gloucester (38 miles/61 km from Boston) is a gritty salty town, the country's oldest fishing port and also the busiest on the Massachusetts coast. Rows of gulls perch on the ridges of the factory roofs that line the wooden quays and jetties, while a steady stream of fishing craft and whale-watch cruisers weigh and drop anchor. It's also home to one of the most engaging small museums anywhere, the **Cape Ann Historical Association.** It shows the largest collection of paintings by native of Gloucester Fitz Hugh Lane (1804–1865) along with works by other artists who visited Cape Ann — Winslow Homer, Milton Avery, and others. It also has exhibits on the Gloucester fishing industry and the area's granite quarrying industry.

From Gloucester take East Main Street south along the harbor towards Eastern Point and visit the fantasy house,

Beauport, which was built by Henry Davis Sleeper a prominent interior designer of the 1920s and 1930s, decorator to such stars as Joan Crawford and Fredric March. See the 40 elaborate rooms displaying historical collections of American and European decorative arts arranged by this genius.

From Gloucester Routes 127 and 127A loop around Cape Ann to **Rockport,** a famous art colony. En route you'll pass the sandy Good Harbor Beach and Long Beach. Rockport's harbor is picturesque, and Motif #1, a red shack covered with brightly colored lobster floats, is one of New England's most painted images — hence its name.

Visitors swamp the port in summer, particularly Bearskin Neck alongside the harbor, which is lined with small gabled and flower-decked huts selling tourist fare — scrimshaw, fudge, leather, pewter, and typical art. When you've finished shopping, ask for The Paper House, a chalet and its contents entirely constructed from 100,000 newspapers.

Gloucester Harbor — the country's oldest fishing port and the busiest on the Massachusetts coast.

Leading Museums and Galleries

Arnold Arboretum, 125 Arborway, Jamaica Plain; Tel. 524-1718. MBTA: Forest Hills. Daily from sunrise to sunset. Exhibits weekdays 9am–4pm, weekends noon–4pm. Free.

Boston Tea Party Ship and Museum, Congress Street Bridge; Tel. 338-1773. MBTA: South Station. Summer 9am–6pm; fall/winter 10am–4pm; closed mid-December–mid-March. Adults $8; students $7; children 4–12 years $4; 3 years and under free.

Bull and Finch Pub (known as Cheers), 84 Beacon Street; Tel. 227-9605. MBTA: Arlington. Daily 11am–2am. Free.

Bunker Hill Monument, Charlestown; Tel. 242-5641. No. 92 and 93 bus from Haymarket/MBTA: North Station. Daily 9am–5pm. Free

Children's Museum, 300 Congress Street, Waterfront; Tel. 426-8855; www.bostonkids.org. MBTA: South Station. Fun and didactic "hands-on" museum. Its most original feature is an entire Japanese house. 10am–5pm Saturday–Thursday; 10am–9pm Friday; Admission $7; $2-$6 concessions; 5–9pm Friday $1 for everyone. (See page 44)

Harvard University Art Museums, entrances at 485 Broadway (at Quincy Street), 32 Quincy Street, 11 Divinity Avenue, and 24 Quincy Street. For times and hours: www.artmuseums.harvard.edu and www.peabody.harvard.edu; Arthur M. Sackler Museum (Classical, Asian,and Islamic art): Tel 495-9400; Fogg Museum (European/North American art) and Busch-Reisinger Museum (German art): Tel 495-2397; Peabody Museum: Tel 496-1027; Sert Gallery: Tel 495-9400. (See pages 59–60)

Isabella Stewart Gardner Museum, 280 The Fenway; Tel. 566-1401. MBTA: Museum. A collection of masterpieces including Titian, Raphael and Veronese, idiosyncratically displayed in a beautiful mansion. 11am–5pm Tuesday–Sunday.

Admission $11; $5-7 concessions; under 18's free. Open many major holidays. (See page 52)

John F. Kennedy Library and Museum, Columbia Point; Tel. 929-4523. MBTA: JFK/Umass and free shuttle. Daily 9am–5pm. Adults $8; seniors and students $6; children aged 13–17 $4.

Longfellow National Historic Site, 105 Brattle Street, Cambridge; Tel. 876-4491. MBTA: Harvard Square. Wednesday–Sunday 8:30am–5pm. Adults and seniors $4.

Massachusetts State House, Beacon Street; Tel. 727-3676. MBTA: Park Street, Monday–Saturday, 10am–5pm. Tours free.

Museum of Fine Arts, 465 Huntington Avenue; Tel: 369-3770 or 369-3306; www.mfa.org. MBTA: Museum. Boston's finest and most comprehensive art and sculpture collection; superb Asian and Egyptian galleries, and rooms full of Impressionist works. One of the most important art c0collections in the country. 10am–4:45pm Monday and Tuesday; 10am–9:45pm Wednesday–Friday; 10am–5:45pm Saturday and Sunday. Admission $1; $5-$10 concessions; under-17s free on weekends and school holidays; children under 6 free. (See page 52)

Museum of Science, Science Park, across Chπarles River; Tel. 723-2500. MBTA: Science Park. This vast complex celebrates science and computer technology and a day trip is recommended. Daily 9am–5pm (Friday 9pm). Adults $10; seniors $7; children 14 and under free. Planetarium and Omni Theater: adults $7.50; seniors/children 14 and under $5.50. (See page 65)

New England Aquarium, at Atlantic Avenue & Milk Street; MBTA Aquarium; Tel: 973-5200. July–Labor Day 9am–6pm Monday, Tuesday, Friday; 9am–8pm Wednesday and Thursday; 9am–7pm Saturday and Sunday; After labor day – 30 June 9am–5pm Monday–Friday; 9am–6pm Saturday and Sunday. Admission $5.50-$12.50. Terrific coral reef tank plus other marine and freshwater habitats; dolphin and sea lion presentations. (See page 43).

Old South Meeting House 310 Washington Street, between Milk and Water Streets; Tel 482-6439; MBTA Downtown Crossing or State. Open 9:30am–5pm daily; Adults $3; students/seniors, and children 6-18 $2. Under 6's free.

Old North Church, 193 Salem Street; Tel. 523-6676. MBTA: Haymarket. Daily 9am–5pm. Free.

Old South Meeting House, 310 Washington Street, between Milk and Water Streets; Tel 482-6439; MBTA Downtown Crossing or State. Open 9:30am–5pm daily; Adults $3; students/seniors, and children 6-18 $2. Under 6's free.

Old State House, 206 Washington Street at State Street, Tel: 720-3290. Bank T. Open 9am–5pm daily. Admission $1-$3.

Paul Revere House, 19 North Square; Tel. 523-2338. MBTA: Haymarket. November 1–April 14, 9:30am–4:15 pm; April 15–October 31, 9:30 am–5:15 pm. Closed Monday January–March. Adults $2.50; students and seniors $2; 5–17 years $1; under 5 years free.

Sports Museum of New England, FleetCenter; Tel. 624-1234. MBTA: North Station. Tuesday–Thursday 10am–5pm, Friday–Saturday 10am–3pm, Sunday noon–5pm. Adults $5; seniors/children 6–17 $4.

U.S.S. Constitution, Charlestown Navy Yard; Tel. 242-5670. MBTA: North Station/ferry from Long Wharf. Daily 9:30am–3:50pm for guided tours, 3:50pm to sunset for self-guided tours of the top deck. Free.

U.S.S.Constitution Museum, Charlestown Navy Yard; Tel: 242-5671. Community College T/ MBTA North Station. Open daily 9:30–3:50pm. Admission is by voluntary contribution.

WHAT TO DO

SHOPPING

The pedestrianized city center around **Downtown Crossing,** along Washington, Winter, and Summer streets, has such major department stores as Filene's and Macy's — as well as a selection of old-fashioned traditional shops scattered along the sidestreets.

Faneuil Hall Marketplace is a great place to shop for gifts; it has many themed boutiques and stalls selling kites, boxer shorts, decorative pigs, hand-made Irish woolens, and a host of other arts and crafts items that makes gift shopping easy. Check out the Boston Pewter Company and the Boston Silver Company, both in the South Market building. See also the merchandise at Celtic Weavers in the North Market Building and the fare at Boston Cooks under the South Canopy of Quincy Market. Disney and Warner Brothers stores are also here.

In Back Bay, the premier shopping areas are Copley Place and Newbury Street. **Copley Place** holds over a hundred shops, many of them top-of-the-line brand-name merchandisers. Look for Neiman Marcus, Coach, Gucci, J. Crew, Bottega Veneta, Bally, Brookstone, Godiva, Joan and David, Montblanc, Polo, and Caswell Massey. It has a few singular stores. Look for the Artful Hand Gallery, which represents hundreds of craftspeople, and Beylerian and Enrico Celli, both men's fashion stores. Two department stores, Lord & Taylor and Saks Fifth Avenue anchor the nearby **Prudential Center.**

Newbury Street is *the* street to shop in Back Bay. Here you can study the eye-catching window displays of the various art galleries, antique shops, and avant-garde, designer boutiques that line the sidewalks. You'll encounter such familiar names as Brooks Brothers, Burberrys, Cole Haan, and Allen Edmonds, plus unique stores like Bijoux at number 141 selling fine women's fashions, and such galleries as Judi Rotenberg representing contemporary American artists at 130, Vose Galleries specializing in 18th- and 19th-century American art, and Qingping Gallery Teahouse which serves tea and sells Asian antiques and artifacts.

If you like to shop, then search no further — Faneuil Hall is the place to be.

In Cambridge, the **CambridgeSide Galleria** contains many chain and fashion stores. **Harvard Square** is the center for student-oriented stores. Don't miss the Harvard Co-op and also the Cambridge Artists Cooperative on Church Street.

The Museum stores are also great sources for gifts. In particular see the stores at the Museum of Fine Arts, the Isabella Stewart Gardner Museum, the Science Museum, the Children's Museum, and the Aquarium.

What to Buy

Art and Antiques: Stroll along Newbury Street to look at the treasures in the well-dressed windows of the galleries and stores. For serious collectors.

Head for Charles Street on Beacon Hill for less expensive but still high-quality china, glass, bric-a-brac, and old prints. The Museum of Fine Arts shop (also in Copley Place) offers fine reproduction sculptures, paintings, and jewelry, as well as books. Those with a car will want to take a trip about 30 minutes north to Essex, on Cape Ann, which has more than 35 antique shops to browse. Most are within walking distance of each other and offer a range of price and quality.

Clothes: Apparel by one of the funkiest designers going can be found at Betsey Johnson at 201 Newbury Street, between Exeter and Fairfield Streets. Or, if you are looking for the latest trends— a jacket from a Massachusetts designer or a dress by a European design house — shop the boutiques on

With over a hundred shops, brand-name outlets, and more, make Copley Place your "next-stop" shopping escapade.

Newbury Street. For bargains, don't miss Filene's Basement (see page 30).

Crafts: Browse the three floors at the Cambridge Artists' Cooperative at 59A Church Street in Cambridge. Prices range from under $10 to the thousands but it's good quality and some of it is whimsical too.

Jewelry: For jewelry in all price ranges shop the Jewelers Exchange, a mini-mall located at 333 Washington Street. The swankiest jeweler's is Tiffany & Company in Copley Place along with such venerable Boston jewelers as Shreve Crump & Low, and Bigelow Kennard, both on Boylston Street.

Music: CDs are generally a better buy here in the US than in Europe. Visit the enormous Tower Records, 360 Newbury Street (at Massachusetts Avenue), or one of the several HMV Stores, as well as the discount stores around Harvard Square.

Seafood: Legal Sea Foods will ship live lobsters to anywhere in the US (for details Tel. 254-7000 or — toll-free in US — 800-343-5804).

Sports: Souvenir shops selling paraphernalia like autographed photos and clothing from all of Boston's major league teams can be found at the arenas (Boston Bruins for example which is in the FleetCenter) and in shopping centers.

Toys: A massive bear gives a wave outside F.A.O. Schwarz, at 440 Boylston Street, Back Bay, the city's best toy shop. Faneuil Hall Marketplace has toy boutiques in addition to a Disney store. The Science and Children's museums also have great stores too.

ENTERTAINMENT

For the latest information on what's happening where during your stay, consult Boston's leading papers and magazines for the range of entertainment listings (see page 113).

The Classical Repertoire

After New York, Boston offers the best and the most **classical music** anywhere in the States. The Boston Symphony Orchestra (known as the BSO) leads the way at Symphony Hall, one of the world's best acoustic venues where seats for the Friday afternoon concerts are the most sought after. In May and June the BSO plays the famous **Boston Pops** series. At the beginning of July, the Pops moves to the Hatch Memorial Shell down at the riverside Esplanade; the performance for the Fourth of July draws many thousands of listeners.

The Berklee College of Music, the New England Conservatory of Music, and the Boston Conservatory all offer full concert schedules. Concerts are also given at the Isabella Stewart Gardner Museum and at the Museum of Fine Arts, both inspiring venues for music. Concerts are also given at the Pickman Concert Hall at the Longy School of Music at Harvard and also at MIT and at the many churches like Trinity, Kings Chapel, and Old South. There are hundreds of smaller chamber and other choral groups performing in the city. See the Handel & Haydn Society for example.

The city has two principal **opera** companies: the Boston Lyric Opera and the Opera Company of Boston. For **dance,** the Boston Ballet performs classical and modern pieces and the Dance Umbrella group is renowned for the high quality of its innovative work. The first performs at the Wang Center for the Performing Arts, the second at the Majestic Theatre.

Theater

Boston has a cluster of theaters on Tremont where most of the Broadway musicals and other Broadway-style shows play at such theaters as the Charles Playhouse, Shubert Theatre, Wilbur Theatre, and Wang Center for the Performing

Arts. At the first, *Shear Madness* — a whodunit set in a Newbury Street hair salon where the audience questions the suspects — is still hosting the longest-running non-musical show in American history. The Colonial Theatre in Back Bay on Boylston Street also hosts Broadway-style shows.

Across the Charles, **The American Repertory Theater/Loeb Drama Center** (Tel: 547-8300) on Brattle Street in Cambridge is one of the best theater companies in the US. Look for such local companies as the American Repertory Theatre and the Huntington Theatre Company.

Comedy

Some of the country's best performers appear in the city's comedy clubs, like the Comedy Connection at Faneuil Hall Marketplace. Try to find out in advance whether well-established professionals or local acts are performing. (The latter are often just as entertaining thanks to their insight into city mores.) Catch the show at the **Comedy Connection** upstairs at Faneuil Hall (Tel: 248-9700) and **Nick's Comedy Stop** at 100 Warrenton Street (Tel: 482-0930). The home the immensely popular ImprovBoston comedy troupe is at the Back Alley Theater on Beacon Street in Cambridge (Tel: 576-1253).

Pay a visit to the Bull and Finch — where "everybody knows your name."

The Late-Night Scene

Cambridge has several great **jazz clubs,** including the **Regattabar** (Tel: 661-5000) in the Charles Hotel and Scullers in the Doubletree Suites, also in Cambridge. Wally's Café on Massachusetts Avenue has hosted the greats from Billie Holiday to Chick Corea and Wynton Marsalis. Telephone the jazz hotline on 787-9700 for additional venues.

For a more raucous time, try the gamut of **clubs** in Boylston Place, off Boylston Street on the edge of Boston Common — The Big Easy, Mercury Bar, Sophia's, the Sugar Shack, and Sweetwater Cafe. If you need a dose of high-energy dancing with a young set, the cavernous clubs in the Entertainment Zone on Lansdowne Road, alongside Fenway Park ballpark, are for you. Avalon (Tel. 262-2424) is one of the largest and most popular nightclubs, and features live music. Bob Dylan, Patti Smith, and James Brown have all played here. Other Lansdowne fixtures include Axis, Karma Club, and Mama Kin.

Thursday night is often the liveliest in **bars,** as many people go away for the weekend. For a sedate, civilized, well-mixed drink go to the Ritz Bar, with its famous martini selection, the Four Seasons Bristol Lounge, the Oak Bar in the Fairmount Copley, or the Julien bar at the Meridien. You can rub shoulders with

Impromptu jazz on Washington Street — music around every corner.

the politicians in Parker's Bar at the Omni Parker House (see page 124). If you like to mix with the hip fashion folks try the bar at Biba (see page 135). Wine lovers should head for Les Zygomates, a cool wine bar at 129 South Street.

You're never far from an **Irish pub.** One of the most atmospheric is the Black Rose, 160 State Street (behind Faneuil Hall Marketplace), with Guinness and nightly live music. Other authentic Irish bars to visit include: Kitty O' Shea's on State Street, The Field on Prospect Street in Cambridge, and the Plough and Stars, also in Cambridge on Massachusetts Avenue. On Beacon Hill, the Bull and Finch Pub (see page 23) which served as the inspiration for the wildly popular sitcom Cheers remains massively popular with visitors. Those seeking a less manic crowd would do well to try Sevens Pub at 77 Charles Street (Tel: 523-9074).

Outdoor Entertainment

In summer, the Boston Pops (see above) and various shows – film, dance, concert – take place at the Hatch Memorial Shell. A band might take over the City Hall Plaza or Copley Square on Friday, when locals settle down for the evening with a deck chair. At any time of year there's a medley of street entertainment, from saxophonists to Beatles singers, jugglers, fire-eaters, and much more around Harvard Square.

SPORTS

Spectator Sports

The **Red Sox** (baseball team) are much loved even though they haven't won a World Series since 1918. It's said that a curse has hung over the club ever since it traded Babe Ruth to the New York Yankees. They play at Fenway Park, 4 Yawley Way; Tel: 267-9440 or 236-6666 daily from April–September.

The **Celtics** (basketball) and the **Bruins** (ice hockey) are as victorious as the Red Sox are unsuccessful, with legendary players like Larry Bird of the Celtics (now coach of the Indiana Pacers) and Bobby Orr of the Bruins. FleetCenter has replaced the arena that witnessed their triumphs, Boston Garden. The Celtics (Tel: 624-1000) play from November to April. The Bruins (Tel: 624-1000) play from October to April.

Although the **New England Patriots** American football team play out of town at the Foxboro Stadium, 25 miles (40 km) south of Boston, every home game is usually sold out. For information call 931–2222 or 800-543–1776. Special trains leave from South Station and Back Bay Station. The season runs from September to December. The soccer team, *New England Revolution*, also plays at Foxboro Stadium.

The oldest annual marathon in the world – the **Boston Marathon** – is held on Patriot's Day (the third Monday in April), while the **Head of the Charles Regatta** takes place on the penultimate Sunday in October, with thousands of spectators lining the Charles River. (The marathon also attracts a huge audience.) Finally, sports fans should visit the New England Sports Museum (see page 79).

Participatory Sports

Boston Harbor is as busy as the city's streets, so you need to be extremely proficient if you want to sail. So long as you are, then pay a visit to the clubs situated on the wharves in Downtown.

Gentler sailing is possible on the Charles River, if you're experienced. Contact Community Boating, behind the Hatch Memorial Shell on the Esplanade; Tel. 523-1038, which offers two-day memberships for $50 and allows experienced sailors, kayakers, and windsurfers to use their equipment. The expensive hotels often have lap pools and fitness centers. The YMCA at 316 Huntington Avenue has extensive health facilities.

Leave those crowded streets behind — smooth sailing on the Charles River.

Put on your running shorts and jog along the Esplanade. If you want to have a go at in-line skating, you can rent equipment at Beacon Hill Skate, 135 Charles Street South; Tel. 482-7400. If you prefer biking, try Back Bay Bicycles, 336 Newbury Street; Tel. 247-2336; or Community Bicycle Supply at 496 Tremont Street, (Tel: 542-8623). The traffic mayhem could easily put you off renting a bike. For winter romance don a pair of skates and take to the ice on the Frog Pond on Boston Common.

CHILDREN

Parents are more likely to have a happy family holiday if they resist the temptation to regard a stay in Boston as one long history lesson. The best stops for children on the Freedom Trail are the *U.S.S. Constitution* and the detour to the Boston Tea Party Museum. On weekends, the National Historical Park and Boston by Foot (see page 109) lay on children's Freedom Trail walking tours.

Boston could hardly be better equipped with museums aimed at children; the Children's Museum, the Aquarium, and the Museum of Science hold most children's (and parents') interest, while the Zoology Museum in Cambridge appeals to young people.

At the Public Garden (see page 22) there is lots for younger children, with gentle rides on the swan boats in summer. Kids also like to pat the quaint *Make Way for Ducklings* statues. The zoo doesn't deserve a visit in its own right: combine it with other sights in the area. Much more exciting is a whale-watching trip (see page 45). Any harbor boat ride is a thrill; take a ferry to Boston Harbor Islands, where you can have a run-around and a swim.

Boston is a city tailor-made for sports-mad kids (not to mention parents). You'll find that at least one major league sports team is playing at any time of year. If you can't see the Bruins or Celtics in action, watch some of the greatest plays on video in the excellent New England Sports Museum (see page 79). Specialist shops all over town sell the teams' uniforms.

Find out what's on at the Puppet Showplace Theater in Brookline (Tel. 731-6400). The *Boston Globe*'s weekly Calendar (see page 113) lists events for children and for teenagers, and the Convention and Visitors Bureau (see page 120) offers the useful *Kids Love Boston* guide and also provides a brochure which details hotels that have family accommodation rates.

Clowning around at Quincy Market — who said Boston is just for grown-ups?

Calendar of events

The Greater Boston Convention and Visitors Bureau publishes biannual travel planners which give the exact dates of all of the city's events and festivals throughout the year.

January. *Chinese New Year* is celebrated in Chinatown. (Sometimes falls in February.)

February. *Boston Festival*: winter festivities featuring ice-sculpting competitions. Often ties in with Valentine's Day celebrations.

March. *St. Patrick's Day*: Irish celebrations are particularly prominent in South Boston ("Southie"), the city's Little Ireland.

April. *Patriot's Day*: re-enactments of the beginnings of the American War of Independence, focusing on Concord and Lexington. The *Boston Marathon* takes place on Patriot's Day (third Monday in April).

May. *Boston Pops*: Boston Symphony Orchestra's two-month summer season begins. *Art Newbury Street*: open house for galleries, and jazz and classical music on the street (also in September). *Annual Kite Festival*: kite-making clinics and kite flying in a festive atmosphere in Franklin Park. *Street Performers Festival*: magicians, jugglers, and musicians take over Faneuil Hall Marketplace.

June. *Bunker Hill Day*: re-enactment of the battle and parade in Charlestown. *Boston Globe Jazz and Blues Festival*: a week of performances, including free midday concerts.

July. *Harborfest*: a week of concerts and special events (such as Chowderfest, a competition to find the city's best clam chowder, and the turnaround of the *U.S.S. Constitution*). Culminates with the *Boston Pops*' Fourth of July (Independence Day) concert and fireworks display on the Esplanade at the Hatch Memorial Shell. *Italian Street Festivals*: street parades, food, and entertainment most weekends in the North End (also in August); see page 35)

October. *Columbus Day*: parade in East Boston or North End. *Head of the Charles Regatta*: enormous one-day rowing event.

December. *Boston Tea Party Re-enactment*: at both the Tea Party Museum and Old South Meeting House. *First Night*: citywide New Year's Eve celebrations.

EATING OUT

Notes on Dining

Unless you want to pay a high price for **breakfast,** don't dine at your hotel. Instead, walk around the corner to either a deli or a coffee shop and pick up something there. Chains like Au Bon Pain are also pleasant spots to indulge in coffee and a croissant. **Brunch** is a combination lunch/breakfast that is served on weekends only. This can be a gargantuan affair at the top hotels like the Four Seasons and the Ritz Carlton but it's worth it. At **lunchtime** do as the Bostonians do and grab a cup of chowder at Quincy market or a massive sandwich or salad at any of the many takeout emporiums. If you enjoy sitting down for a more formal lunch there are plenty of options and the tab will be a lot less than it would be at dinner. **Afternoon tea** (complete with Devonshire clotted cream) can be enjoyed at such places as the Four Seasons and the Ritz Carlton. Both are pricey, but tea is such an ultimate luxury that most of us have long given up, why not indulge? **Dinner** can range in price from very little to a lot depending on where you choose to eat (see the list of Recommended Restaurants beginning on page 132). Bostonians are not late-nighters and most restaurants stop serving at 9:30 or 10 pm. If you're looking for **late-night dining** your best bet is Chinatown or around Harvard Square. **Reservations** are recommended for dinner although there are some places that are very popular that do not take reservations where you should go early or late if you want to avoid a long wait. Note that certain neighborhoods are gaining a reputation for food, particularly the **South End** where new bistros and ethnic spots are springing up every day. Go take a look. The **North End** is of course famous for its

Italian restaurants and cafés. Many cafés with outdoor dining are also found along **Newbury Street.**

Note that while Boston has become more relaxed recently it is still one of the United States' more formal cities and some restaurants still have a jacket and tie rule (Locke Ober, for instance.) Note also that most, if not all, restaurants are non-smoking.

The Cuisine

For many people New England cuisine is seafood, seafood, and seafood, and certainly lobster, crabs, clams, and oysters are traditional fare. The region after all produces Wellfleet oysters, Maine lobster, and the whole city of Boston was founded on the cod, which is why a wooden Sacred Cod

Seafood, seafood, seafood — three reasons why a wooden Sacred Cod hangs in the Massachusetts State House.

hangs in the House of Representatives in the State House. The clambake is a traditional New England feast consisting of clams, lobster, sausage, chicken, potatoes, and corn that is steamed over hot rocks under a covering of seaweed. Don't miss the great New England chowder, which should be served piping hot, brimming with clams and rich with the flavor of the ocean, potatoes, and cream. Many a New Englander will search their entire lives for the ultimate chowder, and you can begin your quest right here in Boston at such restaurants as Turner's. There are plenty of seafood houses serving such fresh fish cooked in a variety of ways. The most successful and most reliable is Legal Seafoods.

Old-fashioned New England cuisine also meant Boston beans and Yankee pot roast and other hearty dishes. These

For a bite on the run — Fenway Park is the perfect place for a traditional hot dog or two.

can still be found but less easily, except at such landmarks as Durgin Park and Parker's at the Omni Parker House. Locke-Ober is another Boston landmark worth visiting if you're a first time visitor to Boston. It's all rather formal and impressive, from the aproned waiters to the German silver tureens and the brass-studded leather chairs. It's one place where you can still sample Indian pudding.

At breakfast seize the opportunity to try some of New England's terrific maple syrup harvested from Vermont and New Hampshire and poured over pancakes or waffles. Traditional egg dishes are available too, but real maple syrup is a treat not to be missed.

At lunch or dinner in season look for such traditional ingredients as sweet corn, cranberries, pumpkin, and blueberries all of which are native to New England. At breakfast you can enjoy cranberry, blueberry, and corn muffins. The sweet corn in summer is a real treat — so sweet and delicious it's even good without butter. Pumpkin is traditionally eaten at the Thanksgiving table for dessert in a special pie flavored with cinnamon, ginger, nutmeg, and cloves. Other traditional desserts are Boston cream pie and Indian pudding. The first is a sponge cake filled with custard and coated with chocolate icing. The second is made with cornmeal and molasses. Both are hard to find today in Boston except at the most traditional restaurants.

In recent years New England cuisine has been transformed by such young chefs as Todd English at Olives, Lydia Shire and Susan Regis at Biba, Chris Schlesinger at East Coast Grill, and Frank McClelland at L'Espalier. These chefs have taken the traditional local ingredients and given them a new twist using French, Italian, or Asian techniques, herbs and spices to produce a truly innovative cuisine. Go to at least one of these restaurants if you can.

The Drinks

Bostonians appreciate their beer and there are several brew-pubs that are producing local brews. The most famous is Samuel Adams. In Cambridge try the ales fashioned by the Cambridge Brewing Company on Kendall Square. Back Bay Brewing Company on Boylston makes great stout too. Many restaurants have excellent wine lists offering selections from all over the world.

Law prohibits "Happy Hours" — when reduced-price drinks are offered. Instead, many bars lure customers with complimentary appetizers. Legal drinking age is 21 (you may be asked for photo identification proving your date of birth, a passport for non-US citizens). For information on the best bars in town, see page 86.

Watching the world drift by — Fort Point Channel provides well needed respite from the wear and tear of Boston.

HANDY TRAVEL TIPS

An A–Z Summary of Practical Information

A

ACCOMMODATION (see also Youth Hostels, and the list of Recommended Hotels beginning on page 123)

The Greater Boston Convention and Visitors Bureau (see Tourist Information) can provide an up-to-date list of accommodations in the city (remember to add a 12.45 percent tax to the rates). It is imperative to book ahead, regardless of the season, because Boston attracts a great number of conventions and the numerous colleges mean that rooms are frequently in demand by parents for special campus events.

Hotels. Downtown Boston hotels are expensive, and additional charges for parking make them even more expensive. The least expensive lodgings are located in the suburbs that ring Downtown. You will, however, need a car if you stay outside town.

Bed & Breakfast. This is less expensive than staying at a hotel and often more fun because your host will help clue you in to the city. Few B&Bs take direct bookings; most use a reservations agency, and accept a booking for a minimum of two nights. Agencies thoroughly vet the B&Bs on their lists, ensuring good standards. Some of the accommodation is superbly located downtown in the waterfront area, Beacon Hill, or the South End, but the majority are located out in suburbs like Brookline. The cost varies enormously, as does the level of comfort and privacy. Note many B&Bs have a complete no-smoking policy. Try the following:

A B&B Agency of Boston, 47 Commercial Wharf, Boston, MA 02110; Tel. (617) 720-3540/800-248-9262 (toll-free in US); fax (617) 523-5761; www.boston-bnagency.com which has downtown homes plus fully furnished apartments and even accommodation on yachts in the harbor.

Bed & Breakfast Associates Bay Colony PO Box 57166, Babson Park Branch, Boston, MA 02157; Tel: 781-449-5301 or 800-347-5088; Fax: 449-5958; www.bnbboston.com. Listings accommodations in B&B's, Inns, suites, and furnished apartments all in a variety of desirable locations throughout Boston. This agency also lists similar accommodations on Cape Cod and throughout Eastern Massachusetts.

New England Bed and Breakfast PO Box 9100, Suite 176, Newton Center, MA 02159; Tel: 244-2112. Small, efficient agency offering home stays in throughout the Boston suburbs. Provides excellent care for those seeking special needs accommodations (pets, no smoking, allergies, etc).

It would be a pity not to stay at least one night in one of the many B&B inns on **Cape Cod** and the **North Shore**. Secure a copy of the *Massachusetts Bed & Breakfast Guide* from the Massachusetts Office of Travel and Tourism (see TOURIST INFORMATION). For luxury B&B Inns on Cape Cod, you can also try:*DestiNNations*, 572 Route 28, West Yarmouth, MA 02673; Tel. (978) 790-0566 or 800-333-INNS (toll-free in US); fax (978) 790-0565.

AIRPORT

Logan International Airport is only 3 miles (5 km) northeast of the city center. A big, busy national and international hub, it has five terminals, where you'll find information desks, currency exchanges, duty-free shops, restaurants, and shops. Call 800-235-6426 (toll-free in US) for information to and from the airport. A frequent shuttle bus service runs between the subway and terminals. Different shuttles serve different terminals, so be sure to get on the right one.

By far the cheapest and quickest way to get to and from the airport is by **the T** (see PUBLIC TRANSPORTATION). The journey from Government Center to the airport stop on the Blue Line takes about

10 minutes, costs under a $1, and operates from 5:30am to 1am. The journey by **road** through the harbor tunnels can be subject to traffic jams, particularly at rush hour — a **taxi** ride from Downtown to the airport can take anything from 10 to 45 minutes. Delays add to the cost, making sharing a taxi common. **Minibus** services run regularly from all major Back Bay and Downtown hotels. A regular **ferry** shuttle (Mon–Fri 6am–8pm every 15 minutes; Friday evening 8–11pm every 30 minutes; Sat 10am–11pm every 30 minutes; Sun 10–8pm every 30 minutes) plies across Boston Harbor from Rowes Wharf to the airport and provides the most exhilarating way of arriving or departing. It takes seven minutes, connecting with a shuttle bus that circuits the terminals in 10 minutes. It's $10 for adults, $5 for seniors, and free for children under 12. Discounted roundtrip available for $17.

B

BOSTON CITIPASS

The Boston CitiPass ticket booklet covers admission to the Museum of Science, New England Aquarium, Skywalk Observatory, Harvard Museum of Natural History, Museum of Fine Arts Boston, and the John F. Kennedy Library and Museum for a flat fee. CitiPasses are good for 9 days, and may be purchased at any of the 6 attractions covered by the pass. (Tel: 707-256-0490, www.citypass.com)

BUDGETING FOR YOUR TRIP

Boston is not the most expensive city in the United States but it's close.

Accommodation rates range from about $170 per night at the Holiday Inn to $475 at the Four Seasons. It's getting hard to find a room downtown for less than $200. Less expensive options are B&Bs (around $100 per night), the Y, and Youth Hostels ($66 in a private room).

Meals: if you want to save money don't take breakfast at your hotel unless it's included. Lunch is always less expensive than dinner and depending on where you choose to eat can range from $2 for a slice of pizza to $35–$40 at l'Aujourd'hui. Dinner can range from $20 at a Chinese or similar ethnic restaurant to $35 at a typical bistro, to $60 plus at the Ritz Carlton.

Transportation: air fares to Boston are least expensive in spring, fall, and winter off-peak periods and most expensive during the summer and major holidays like Christmas and Easter. If you want to save the most money you're advised to shop the bucket shops operated by consolidators who sell discounted fares even during peak season. Some airlines and major tour operators offer all-inclusive flight and accommodation "city breaks," and these are often cheaper than making separate purchases.

To get from the airport to the city, the least expensive way (under $1) is via the **subway (T),** which links to a free shuttle bus to the various terminals; **taxis** are the most expensive (between $10 and $15), and shared limousine or water shuttle is in between at under $10.

Subway Transportation within Boston will cost you 85¢ per ride although your best bet is to buy a special visitor pass allowing you unlimited travel. It costs $5 for one day, $9 for three days, and $18 for 7 days.

Entertainment and Incidentals

A trolley tour will cost around $25; a whale watch around $30. The top rated museums charge $10–$12 admission. Note though that some have discounted admission at certain times on certain days. Only two sights along the Freedom Trail charge admission. For theater performances expect to pay anywhere from $10 to $60; for classical musical concerts $20–$50; opera $30 to $110. Most other incidentals will cost less in the United States than in Europe.

C

CAMPING

Suprisingly enough you can actually camp on four of the Boston Harbor islands. They offer free "wilderness" camping — with no fresh water, for example. You need a permit; call Harbor Islands State Park, Tel. 727-7676 for Lovells and Peddocks islands, and the Department of Environmental Management; Tel. (781) 740-1605 ext. 201 or 205, for Bumpkin and Grape islands.

CAR RENTAL/HIRE (see also DRIVING and MONEY)

Only consider renting a car if you want to take excursions. To rent a car, you must be over 21 years old (a surcharge may be levied if you are under 25), and possess a current driving license. Visitors from non-English-speaking countries may need a translation of their national driving license as well as the original document itself. Rental agencies take credit cards, and many will not rent to people who do not have major credit cards unless they have a verifiable telephone listing and address in their own name.

Major car rental agencies include **Alamo** (Tel: 800-327-9633); **Avis** (Tel: 800-831-2847); **Budget**: (Tel 800-527-0700); **Dollar** (Tel: 800-800-4000); and **Hertz** (Tel: 800-654-3131) which have offices in downtown Boston, Cambridge, and at Logan Airport. Rates can vary, so shop around for the best prices — and don't forget to ask about any drop-off charges if you don't return it to the original rental office. (You may be asked to choose between returning the car with a full tank of gas, or paying for a full tank in advance and returning the car with an empty tank. If you opt for the former, you will probably save some money, but make sure that you fill up before the return or you will end up paying an inflated price for gas at the rental company.) Your own auto insurance plus the insurance provided if you pay with certain credit cards, may provide all the coverage you need for a rental car, but contact your insurance company before rejecting the car rental company's insurance. Usually collision is covered by your own auto insurance or by the credit card company. Liability though may not be covered, although a car booked from abroad will have some third-party liability insurance (check how much with your travel agent). If you consider it inadequate, car-rental agencies offer extended third-party liability protection for an extra charge. Lastly, be sure to establish whether the rental agreement includes free unlimited mileage. A compact car for a week will average $179 plus $17 a day for collision and $10 a day for liability.

CLIMATE

Boston's weather is nothing if not changeable. Here air masses from Canada and the Great Lakes collide with temperate Gulf Stream currents, and erratic weather patterns are influenced by the multiple air masses operating throughout the region. Fall and spring in Boston are magnificent, while its summers can be oppressively steamy. While the city's winter winds can sometimes rival those of Chicago, recent years have seen unusually mild winters, and snowfall is measured in inches and not feet. Fall is famous in New England for the beautiful colors of the turning foliage. The time for this in Boston is mid-to-late October. The chart below gives Boston's average minimum and maximum monthly temperatures:

	J	F	M	A	M	J	J	A	S	O	N	D
Max.°F	36	37	43	54	66	75	80	78	71	62	49	40
°C	2	3	6	12	19	24	27	25	22	17	9	4
Min. °F	20	21	28	38	49	58	63	62	55	46	35	25
°C	-7	-6	-2	3	9	14	17	17	13	8	2	-4

CLOTHING

Pack clothes to contend with erratic weather. In winter, bring a warm coat, hat, gloves, and boots. In summer, tourist wear is a T-shirt and shorts, but don't forget to bring a raincoat and sweater for cooler days, evenings, and boat trips. Though Boston is a laid-back city, in the evening people look casually smart, more so Downtown and in Back Bay than in Cambridge, so pack a jacket and tie for the more formal places. Good comfortable walking shoes are essential.

COMPLAINTS

If you feel you have a serious complaint about a business, and the manager of the establishment has not resolved the problem to your satisfaction, contact the Executive Office of Consumer Affairs and Business Regulation, 1 Ashburton Pl., Room 1411, Boston, MA 02108; Tel. 727-7780.

CRIME AND SAFETY (see also EMERGENCIES and POLICE)

Compared to many other American cities, Boston is relatively safe. Here, everyone uses the subway and walks the streets until late at night.

However, after dark you should avoid Boston Common and the Public Garden, the Esplanade along the river, and the Combat Zone (along Washington Street between Stuart and Avery), the southern end of the South End, and parts of the southern suburbs — Roxbury and Jamaica Plain. You can reduce the risk of theft with a few precautions: Always lock your hotel room and car (the state has a surprisingly high level of car crime); wear a minimum of jewelry; and never leave bags and valuables unattended.

CUSTOMS AND ENTRY REQUIREMENTS

Most people need visas to visit the US. The exceptions are as follows: Canadians who need evidence of their nationality (which is ideally a passport); the British, citizens of the republic of Ireland, Australia, and New Zealand who need a passport (unless they're staying more than 90 days when they need a visa) and a return air ticket. Citizens from elsewhere need a visa — check current information with your local US consulate or embassy and allow a minimum of three weeks for delivery.

US health authorities require no vaccinations, unless, of course, you are coming from known cholera or yellow fever areas.

Customs limitations are as follows (if you are over 21): 200 cigarettes **or** 50 cigars **or** 2kg tobacco, 1 l of wine **or** spirits, plus $100 worth of gifts. Both arriving and departing passengers should report any money and checks exceeding $10,000.

D

DRIVING

Americans drive on the right and there is little that will surprise anyone who drives in western countries. Boston is currently undergoing the Big Dig, which is creating havoc for downtown drivers. In fact, you're best off not driving in the city. Walk and use public transportation instead. Outside the city the roads are good and fast (expect to pay tolls on the Massachusetts Turnpike and similar interstates so keep some change handy). If you're headed for Cape Cod or the North Shore avoid leaving on Friday and returning on Sunday unless you want to sit in traffic.

Rules and Regulations: The most important rules to observe are the wearing of seatbelts in front and back seats, speeding restrictions (55mph or 88km/h on highways, 65mph or 105km/h on turnpikes) not driving while intoxicated, and parking regulations. Penalties (including towing) are stiff. Rotaries (circles/roundabouts) are common (give way to traffic already on the rotary); look out for signs telling traffic to give way to pedestrians; don't pass school buses (painted yellow) *in either direction* when passengers are getting off *or on* (indicated on the bus by flashing red signal lights). At most traffic lights you can turn right on a red signal after stopping, unless a sign states to the contrary.

Fuel Costs: Gas (petrol) is much cheaper in the United States than elsewhere in the world. Expect to pay from $1.30 and up for regular 87-octane gas. Self-service stations are usually cheaper than full service stations.

Parking: It can be impossible to find on-street parking Downtown or in exclusive neighborhoods such as Beacon Hill where virtually all spaces are for residents only. Establish in advance what parking facilities your hotel can offer (most hotels and smart restaurants have valet parking). There are a number of large underground parking lots throughout the city: Ask the hotel concierge for details.

If You Need Help: It's worth joining your local equivalent of the American Automobile Association, which has reciprocal agreements in many countries. AAA provides emergency towing service plus touring information including maps. For information contact the AAA at 1050 Hingham Street, Rockland, MA 02370; Tel. (617) 781-871-5880. For emergency road service, phone 800-AAA-HELP (617-222-8252).

Road signs. These are generally familiar but foreign visitors may be unfamiliar with the following two road signs.

Divided highway	Dual carriageway
Rotary	Circle/Roundabout

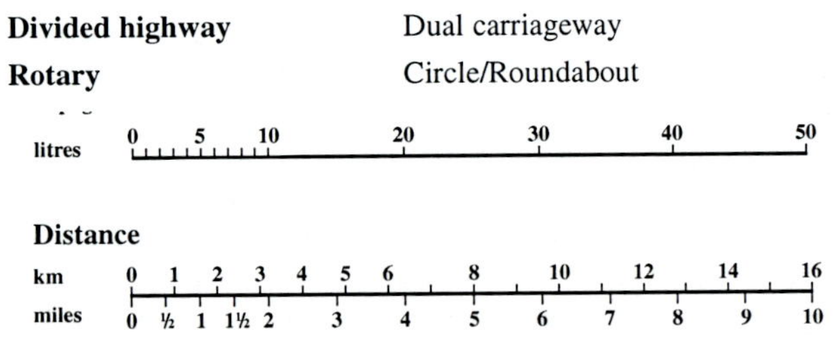

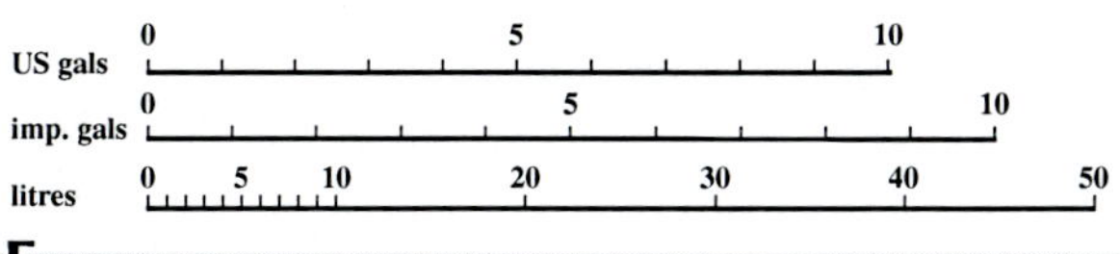

E

ELECTRICITY

The US uses 110-volt 60-cycle AC. Plugs are generally small, flat, and two-pronged, or three-pronged with flat and round pins. Visitors from overseas will need an adapter.

EMBASSIES AND CONSULATES

Australia: Suite 457, Statler Building, 20 Park Plaza, Boston, 02116; Tel. 542-8655.

Canada: (Consulate) Suite 400, 3 Copley Place, Boston, MA 02116; Tel. 262-3760.

Republic of Ireland: (Consulate) 535 Boylston Street, Boston, MA 02116; Tel. 267-9330.

New Zealand: The closest embassy is in Washington at 37 Observatory Circle; NW, DC 20008; Tel. (202) 328-4800.

South Africa: The closest consulate is in New York at 333 East 38th Street, 9th Floor, New York, NY 10016; Tel. (212) 213-4880.

United Kingdom: (Consulate) Federal Reserve Plaza, 25th Floor, 600 Atlantic Avenue, Boston, MA 022110; Tel. 248-9555.

EMERGENCIES (see also HEALTH AND MEDICAL CARE and POLICE)

Dial **911** for police, ambulance, or the fire department. For a doctor, telephone **859-1776.**

G

GAY AND LESBIAN TRAVELERS

Given the large student population, Boston is fairly open to gay men and lesbians. The city's gay community is focused in South End. Visitors can secure information from the **Helpline** at 267-9001 (weekdays 6–11pm, Sat 5–7:30pm, Sun 5–10pm) and also from the *in newsweekly*, New England's largest gay and lesbian newspaper, published every Thursday. Provincetown on Cape Cod is one of the premier gay beach resorts in the nation.

GETTING THERE (see also AIRPORTS and BUDGETING FOR YOUR TRIP)

Air Travel

From the United States and Canada. Direct flights operate from all major US cities to Boston. Major airlines run shuttle services from Chicago and New York, and there are frequent direct flights from Montréal and Toronto. There are also direct flights from Ottawa, Halifax, Québec City, and Vancouver.

From the UK. Major airlines fly direct daily from Gatwick and Heathrow (non-stop London to Boston takes 7 to 8 hours). There is also direct service from Manchester. Airlines also operate from Bristol, Birmingham, Leeds, Aberdeen, Edinburgh, and Glasgow connecting either via Heathrow or Brussels.

From the Republic of Ireland. There are direct flights from Shannon and Dublin; the journey takes approximately 7 to 7 ½ hours. Other flights are routed via John F. Kennedy or Heathrow and Gatwick.

From Australia and New Zealand. Airlines fly via San Francisco or Los Angeles from Sydney, Melbourne, and Auckland. Flying time from Sydney is 20 to 24 hours; from Melbourne 27 to 32 hours;

from Auckland 19 to 40 hours depending on the flight and routing chosen.

From South Africa. South African Airways operates from Cape Town via Atlanta and from Johannesburg via New York Kennedy. Depending on the airline, flights from Johannesburg are routed via London Heathrow, Miami, or Brussels. Flying time from Johannesburg to Boston is 20–30 hours.

Rail Travel

Amtrak links Washington, DC, Philadelphia, New York, and Chicago to Boston. High-speed service between DC and Boston is scheduled to debut in 2000 cutting the trip between Washington and Boston to four hours. Trains arrive at South Station or Back Bay, which are connected directly to the T. For information in the US and Canada, call 800-USA-RAIL (toll-free) or (617) 482-3660. Amtrak has representatives in all major countries. Rail passes for unlimited travel within a set period are offered to foreign visitors: the Coastal and Eastern Rail Pass includes Boston.

Bus Travel

Greyhound, Tel. 800-231-2222 (toll-free in US), links Boston to all major cities in North America. Foreign travelers can purchase an Ameripass (it must be bought outside the US) for unlimited travel within a set period. Phone the Greyhound representative in your own country.

Car Travel

Boston is 215 miles (346 km) from New York, 439 miles (706 km) from Washington, DC, and 965 miles (1553 km) from Chicago.

GUIDES AND TOURS

Trolley tours. After following the painted red line of the self-guided Freedom Trail (see page 26), the most popular way of seeing Boston is aboard a trolley. Old Town Trolley Tours (orange and green), Beantown Trolleys (red) and Boston Trolley Tours (blue) offer virtually identical

90-minute trips around downtown Boston and its neighborhoods. The narration depends on your guide, but you can always hop on and off along the way. Booths selling tickets are liberally dotted throughout the city. Old Town Trolley Tours offer Cambridge tours too.

For an adventuresome variation, try **Boston Duck Tours**, on which the amphibious "bus" plunges into the Charles River and chugs along the river at the end!

Walking tours: Michel Topor, an authority on Italian food, wine and culture leads walking tours through **Little Italy** on Wednesdays and Saturdays and 10am and 2pm, and on Fridays at 3pm. Reservations are required, Tel. 523-6032. Don Quijote Tours (Tel. 328-1333) conducts daily **foreign language tours** in Spanish, French, Portuguese, and Italian of Boston or outlying areas. **Boston's Parks and Recreation Department Park Rangers** (1010 Massachusetts Avenue; Tel. 635-7383) offer a number of free tours and programs. Free tours of the **Black Heritage Trail** are offered on weekdays at 10am, noon, and 2pm by reservation only. Call the Museum of Afro-American History (Tel. 739-0022) or the Boston African American National Historic Site (Tel. 742-5415) to make reservations 24 hours in advance. Guided tours of a Literary Trail threads through homes, haunts, and landscapes in Boston, Cambridge, and Concord. Tel. 350-0358 for tour information

Excursions. Brush Hill Tours; Tel. 236-2148, offers in-town tours and coach excursions to surrounding areas, including Lexington and Concord, Plymouth, Cape Cod, Salem, and the North Shore.

Cruises. Companies offer harbor tours, sunset cruises, dinner cruises; and whale watches. **Boston Harbor Cruises,** Long Wharf; Tel. 227-4321: harbor, sunset, and whale-watch trips. Also water shuttle to Charlestown Naval Yard. **Bay State Cruise Company,** Long Wharf; Tel. 748-1428: day trips to Provincetown (from Commonwealth Pier), whale watch, sunset, inner harbor, outer harbor, JFK Museum trips. Also ferry to Georges Island and a free inter-island service. **AC Cruise Line,** 290 Northern Avenue; Tel. 261-6633 or toll-free 800-422-8419: day trips to Gloucester, whale watch. *Spirit of Boston,* Rowes Wharf; Tel. 748-1499, and Odyssey Cruises, Rowes Wharf; Tel. 654-9700, offer luncheon and dinner cruises. **Whale watches** are offered by Boston Harbor Whale Watch, Rowes Wharf; Tel. 345-9866, and New England Aquarium Whale Watch, Central Wharf; Tel. 973-5281. A 50-minute cruise up and down the **Charles** with Charles River Boat Company; Tel. 621-3001, from CambridgeSide Galleria and the Museum of Science, is a pleasant, sedate experience.

H

HEALTH AND MEDICAL CARE

The quality of health care is the most advanced in the world, but you will have to pay for it and it will be extraordinarily expensive. Therefore make sure that you have taken out adequate travel insurance via a travel agent or insurance company before you leave home. If you need special drugs or medicines, bring them with you and make sure you have detailed medical backup information with you in case you lose them. Some medicines sold over the counter abroad are available by prescription only in the US — check with your doctor. **CVS Drugstore,** 155 Charles Street; Tel. 523-4372 or 523-1028, opens daily 8am–midnight.

Hospital emergency rooms will treat anyone in need of immediate medical attention.

Beth Israel Hospital: 330 Brookline Avenue; Tel. 667-8000 (667-3337 for emergencies).

Cambridge City Hospital: 1493 Cambridge Street; Tel. 498-1000.

Massachusetts General Hospital: 55 Fruit Street; Tel. 726-2000.

HOLIDAYS

Banks, businesses, and some stores are closed on the following days (except where otherwise indicated).

January 1	*New Year's Day*
Third Monday in January*	*Martin Luther King Day*
Third Monday in February*	*Presidents Day*
Third Monday in April**	*Patriots Day*
Last Monday in May	*Memorial Day*
July 4	*Independence Day*
First Monday in September	*Labor Day*
Second Monday in October*	*Columbus Day*
November 11*	*Veterans Day*
Fourth Thursday in November	*Thanksgiving Day*
December 25*	*Christmas Day*

*shops open
** some shops and businesses open; banks open am

L

LANGUAGE

Most English-speaking foreigners are familiar with American words and phrases, but here are a few that may cause confusion.

US	*British*
bill	banknote
check	bill (restaurant)
faucet	tap
first floor/2nd floor	ground floor/first floor

pants	trousers
purse/pocketbook	handbag
suspenders	braces
underpass	subway
undershirt	vest
vest	waistcoat

LOST PROPERTY

If you lose something on the MBTA, phone **722-3200**. If you lose something in a cab, call the cab company and check with the Boston Police Department to see if it has been handed in.

M

MAPS

Maps are readily available. We like the laminated Streetwise series, which has a street index. If you need a detailed map of the state that shows every road and every elevation then purchase one of the atlases in the DeLorme series.

MEDIA

Newspapers and magazines. The city has two main papers, *The Boston Herald*, a tabloid, and *The Boston Globe*. Look for the "The Calendar," in the Thursday edition of the *Globe* and the "Night & Day" section on Sunday for entertainment listings. *The Herald* has listings in its Friday edition.

Among the weeklies the most thorough, for reviews and listings, is the weekly *Boston Phoenix* (Friday). *The Improper Bostonian* is also good, with lots of suggestions for things to do. The free monthly *Where Boston/Cambridge* magazine details shops, restaurants, and entertainment. The monthly *Boston Magazine* is more critical, notably in its famous, fun, and influential Best and Worst annual review of everything the city offers.

Out of Town News in Harvard Square, Cambridge, has a wide selection of national and international publications.

Radio and Television. Both AM and FM have good radio stations playing both popular and classical music. Every hotel room has a TV (B&Bs often don't), with a choice of network and cable channels. The main network channels are: channel 4 (CBS); channel 5 (ABC); channel 7 (NBC); channel 2 and 44 for PBS (Public Broadcasting Service which carries no ads). The most useful cable channels are CNN (Cable News Network) for nonstop news, the Weather Channel for national and local forecasts, MTV (Music TV), and ESPN for sports.

MONEY

Today the easiest and often the least expensive way to obtain money abroad is from an ATM machine using either your bank or credit card.

Currency. The dollar is divided into 100 cents (¢). *Banknotes*: $1 (a buck), $5, $20, $50, $100. All notes are the same size and color, so beware of mixing them up. *Coins*: 1¢ (penny), 5¢ (nickel), 10¢ (dime), 25¢ (quarter), $1.

Exchange facilities. Use ATMs or change cash and traveler's checks at banks. If you bring traveler's checks bring them in dollar denominations they're hard to exchange otherwise.

Credit cards. Plastic is used everywhere. Use your credit card to secure cash at bank cash machines (be sure to check with your bank for details).

Traveler's checks. Banks will exchange them for cash without a charge (take ID with you). Most establishments accept them as payment, but $20 checks are the most useful for such transactions. Keep your checks in the hotel safe and a note of their serial numbers in a separate place.

Tax. Advertised prices do not include tax. The Massachusetts State sales tax is 5.7 percent, levied on everything except medicine, store-bought food, and clothes under $175. Hotel tax is 12.45 percent.

OPEN HOURS (see also PUBLIC HOLIDAYS)

Stores. Generally, stores open Monday to Saturday from 9am or 10am to 5:30 or 7pm and Sunday from noon to 5 or 6pm. Some stores stay open much longer. Shopping malls may stay open Monday to Friday until 9 or 9:30pm, and on Sunday afternoons.

Banks. Most banks open Monday to Friday 9am to 3 or 4pm (or later), and Saturday 9am to noon or 2pm, but be sure to check with you local branch.

Restaurants. Boston is not a late-night town like New York and most restaurants stop serving food as early as 10pm.

POLICE

In an emergency, phone **911**. Police, wearing dark blue, are generally very approachable. Their presence is very visible — on foot, horseback, bicycle, motorbike, and in cars. They also patrol the MBTA.

POST OFFICES

The United States Postal Service only deals with mail. Post office opening hours vary; most open Monday to Friday 8am to 5pm, and Saturday 9am to 1pm. Hotels and shops also sell stamps. Collection times are marked on Boston's mailboxes (blue with a red-and-white logo).

The General Post Office, 25 Dorchester Avenue, Boston, MA 02205, Tel. 654-5225, is located behind South Station. Currently it costs 33 cents to mail a letter within the US, 55 cents for a one-ounce letter to Canada or Mexico, and 60 cents to anywhere else in the world. Post cards cost 55 cents (45 cents to Canada and Mexico).

PUBLIC TRANSPORTATION (also Car Rental/Hire, Driving, and Transportation in Budgeting for Your Trip)

The Massachusetts Bay Transportation Authority (MBTA) runs the subway trains, trolleys, buses and commuter trains. Call 222-3200 or 800-392-6100 (toll-free in US) for information.

The Subway or the T. The T is a safe and reliable system of underground and aboveground trains and trolleys. There are four lines — red, green, blue, and orange — with trains colored to match. Stops are marked on the street by the letter T in a circle. If you have a pass you're just waved through; otherwise, buy a token from the booth and deposit it or the exact amount in change in the turnstile at the start of your journey. Platforms are marked "Inbound" — meaning that the train is going in the direction of Park Street or Downtown Crossing — or "Outbound" (to the suburbs). Note that the red and green lines have branches: letters on the front of trains correspond to the branch destinations. Trains start running at 5am (a little later on Sundays), and the last ones leave Downtown around 12:45am. Maps and information are available from the Park Street station. Children between five and eleven travel half price, under-fives for free.

Bus. Buses run on cross-town routes and to outer suburbs (details on the Metro Boston Transit Map). Exact change is required on buses.

Special Passes A subway and bus visitor pass, called the Boston Passport, allows unlimited travel on buses or subways in Boston (1-day $5, 3-day $9, 7-day $18). These passes can be purchased from the Visitor Information Center on Boston Common daily from 9am to 5pm.

Train. Commuter Rail, also known as the Purple Line, goes to the North Shore (it's called the Beach Train) and to Lexington and Concord. There are three city-center stations: North Station (for trains to Concord and the North Shore), South Station, and Back Bay. In all three, you will find maps showing the whole network, and schedules for individual lines.

Taxi. Traveling by taxi is expensive, and because of Boston's traffic, not always the quickest way to go. Taxis can be found waiting outside hotels or around shopping and dining centers like Downtown Crossing and Faneuil Hall Marketplace. If you want to go to somewhere off the beaten track, don't rely on the driver knowing where it is.

For more information, call any of the following: **Checker;** Tel. 536-7000 (Boston)/497-1500 (Cambridge); **Red Cab;** Tel. 734-5000; **Town Taxi;** Tel. 536-5000.

R

RELIGION

Many different denominations worship in Boston, and the city is also the world center for the Christian Science movement. Hotels can provide details of church and synagogue services. The Yellow Pages list places of worship under "Churches" and "Synagogues." Also, the Saturday newspapers give information on Sunday services.

S

SPECIAL NEEDS AND THE DISABLED

The MBTA (Massachusetts Bay Transit Authority) has and excellent web site (www.mbta.com) replete with information about handicapped accessible transportation. Many of the subway ("T") and commuter rail stops are wheelchair accessible. For more information, call the MBTA at 722-5123. The following taxi companies service Boston and neighboring areas, and have wheelchair-accessible transportation available on request, (24 hours notice is suggested if possible). Red & White Cab Assn. (Tel: 242-0800), Independent Taxi Operators Assn. (Tel: 426-8700), and Boston Cab Assn. (Tel: 262-2227). The City of Boston's Disabled Person's Commission can be reached at Tel: 635-3682.

T

TELEPHONE

The country code for the US is **91.**

The area code for Boston is **617.**

Dial the following for:

The operator **0**

Local directory information **411**

Long distance information **1,** then **area code,** then **555-1212**

International dial **011,** then **country code,** then **area code,** then **phone number.**

Emergencies **911**

Numbers with prefixes 800, 888, and 877 are toll-free in the United States and Canada.

Save money by using public phones unless you want to pay the exorbitant surcharges levied by your hotel. The best way to make the call is to purchase a telephone card from any newsstand for $5 or $10 and follow the instructions, or to use a telephone card or credit card.

If you don't use a card then note the following: **Public phones** take 5-, 10-, and 25-cent coins. For **local calls,** first deposit 25¢; wait for the dial tone, then dial the seven-digit number. You may have to deposit more money, depending on the length of your call. For **long-distance calls**, dial the prefix 1, the three-digit area code, and the seven-digit number, and listen to the automatic voice for instructions on how much money to deposit. You may have to add extra during or after your call. For an **international call** to Europe, you have to deposit a large amount of change: the additional cost of a call from your hotel room may be worth it.

TICKETS AND RESERVATIONS

You can go to the box offices of the particular theaters and concert halls for tickets. For credit card bookings, contact **Ticketmaster**, which provides tickets for sporting events, concerts, and performances throughout Boston (Tel: 931-2000, or 931-2787). For baseball, basketball, and hockey games, buy tickets as far in advance in advance as you can. Some standing room or general admission tickets are usually available on the day of play. For half-price, day_of show tickets and information for more than 200 local performance centers, **Bostix** is the place to go. Tickets are sold at 11am on the day of the performance for cash only, (Tel: 482-2849). **Telecharge** sells tickets for the Shubert Theatre and The Wang Center for the Performing Arts, (Tel: 447-7400).

TIME ZONES

Boston is on Eastern Standard Time. From April to October, Daylight Saving Time is adopted and clocks move ahead one hour. The chart below shows winter times.

Los Angeles	**Boston**	London	Johannesburg	Sydney
9am	**noon**	5pm	7pm	4am

TIPPING

In restaurants a service charge is not added to the check so tips are expected. Leave anywhere from 15 to 20 percent depending on the quality of the service. In a bar, you're expected to leave the change from buying a drink on the bar top as a tip (10% on a higher tab). Otherwise tip the following:

Tour guide	10–15 percent
Hairdresser/barber	15 percent
Hotel porter (per bag)	$1–$1.50
Taxi driver	15–20 percent
Waiter/waitress	15–20 percent

TOILETS

It's hard to find public conveniences in Boston. Look for them in shopping malls, large stores, hotel lobbies, and railroad and bus stations and other large public facilities. People often use those in restaurants but some managements frown on this practice so you might have to buy a beverage or some small item.

TOURIST INFORMATION

In Boston: The Greater Boston Convention & Visitors Bureau, Two Copley Place, Suite 105, Boston, MA 02116; Tel. (617) 536-4100 or 888-773-2678; www.bostonusa.com provides numerous brochures including *The Official Guidebook*, *Travel Planner,* and *Kids Love Boston*. A new service, "Boston by phone," is open 24-hours. The service links callers from North America directly to suppliers in seven different fields of interest. Call the 888 number above for access.

Massachusetts Office of Travel and Tourism, 10 Park Plaza, Suite 4510, Boston, MA 02216; Tel: 727-3201; www.massvacation.com

The **Boston Common Visitor Information Center** is on the Tremont Street side of Boston Common (open Mon–Fri 8:30am–5pm, and Sun 9am–5pm). There is also a kiosk in the Prudential Center (open Mon–Fri 8:30am–6pm, Sat 10am–6pm and Sun 11:30am–6pm).

National Park Service Visitor Center, 15 State Street; Tel. 242-5642._Open June–Sept 9am–5pm; Sept–May 9am–5pm daily. It's the best place for information on historical sights along the Freedom Trail. **Cambridge Information Booth**, Harvard Square, Cambridge. No phone. Open 9am–5pm Mon–Sat. **Traveler's Aid Society** 17 East Street at Atlantic Avenue; Tel: 542-7286 Open 8:30am–5pm Mon–Fri. A non-profit agency that has been assisting travelers since 1920.

W

WEB PLANNING AND INFORMATION

www.artsaroundboston.com for information about the city's art scene.

www.cambridge-usa.org is the site of the Cambridge Tourism Office.

www.massport.com is Logan Airport's stellar site for flight and ground transport planning.

www.bostonchefs.com provides details about dining in Boston.

www.TheInsider.com/boston provides extensive information about current goings-on in Boston.

www.bostonphoenix.com is the site of the local paper, and is a good resource for all kinds of information about the city.

www.boston.com/globe is the site of the city's daily paper *The Globe* and another good resource.

WEIGHTS AND MEASURES (see also DRIVING)

The US is one of the last countries in the world to adopt the metric system, and has not yet launched an official changeover program. For UK tourists, the main difference between British and American measures is 1 US gallon = 0.833 British Imperial gallon = 3.8 liters.

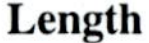

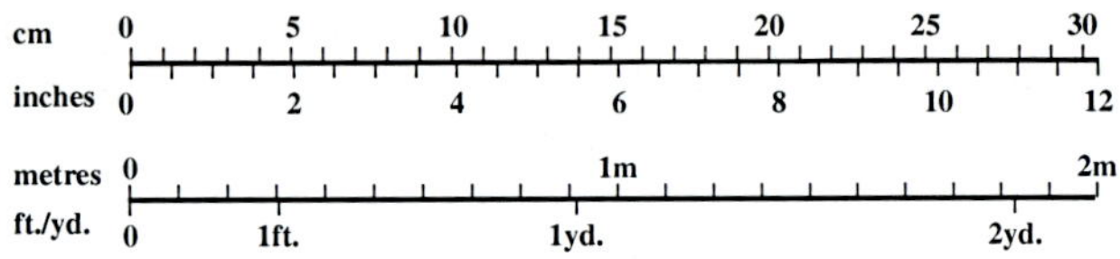

Weight

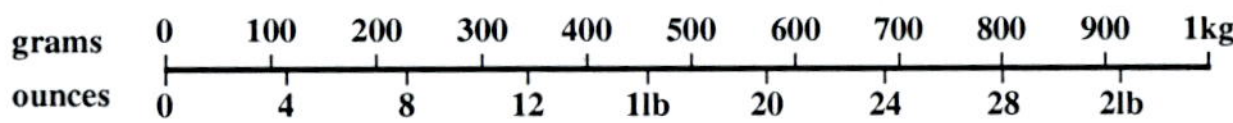

Temperature

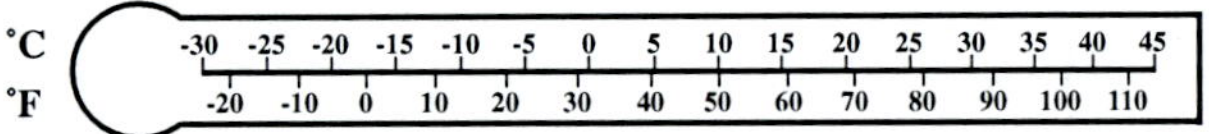

YOUTH HOSTELS

Boston International American Youth Hostel, 12 Hemenway Street, Boston, MA 02115; Tel: 536-1027. Rates are $27-$30 per night in a small six person dorm; $81-87 for private single/double. Breakfast not included. For men: YMCA, 316 Huntington Avenue, Boston, MA 02115 at Northeastern University; Tel: 536-7800. For men: Singles are $45 and doubles are $65. For women: YWCA/Berkeley Residence, 40 Berkley Street, Boston, 02116; Tel: 375-2524. Singles are $56, doubles $86, and triples $99.Florence Frances Guest House, 458 Park Drive, Boston, 02115; Tel: 267-2458. Rates for this four room, 150 year old guest house are $80 for singles and $90 for doubles. Breakfast not included.

Recommended Hotels

Boston accommodations are expensive and they're hard to come by. For cheaper lodging, try Bed & Breakfast establishments (see page 98), and youth hostels and Y's (see page 122). The city has no low season, except maybe January and so reservations are imperative. The price categories below are guides only based on rack rates for a double room excluding 12.45 percent tax. Note that rates do fluctuate from day to day based on room availability so always ask for the absolutely lowest price. Hotels take all major credit cards. Exceptions are noted.

$$$$	above $300
$$$	$200–300
$$	$125–200
$	below $125

BEACON HILL

Beacon Hill Hotel and Bistro $$$$ *25 Charles Street, Boston, MA 02114; Tel: 888-959-2442; www.beaconhillhotel.com.* This elegant 12 room 1 suite hotel is a converted 1830's town house. Opened in 2000, the hotel's amenities include 24-hour room service and a charming French bistro where full breakfasts (included in the rates) are served.

Holiday Inn Government Center $$-$$$ *5 Blossom Street, Boston, MA 02114; Tel: 762-7630 or 800-HOLIDAY.* Situated three blocks from Faneuil Hall and the Financial District. Many of its recently 303 rooms offer picturesque views of Boston. Outdoor pool, express checkout, 24-hour fitness center and 24-hour currency exchange. On site,

Foster's Bar and Grille serves breakfast, lunch, and dinner and features seafood, pasta, and grill selections.

FINANCIAL DISTRICT AND GOVERNMENT CENTER

Le Meridien $$$$ *250 Franklin Street, Boston, 02110; Tel 451-1900 or 800-543-4300; Fax: 423-2844.* Luxurious 326-room hotel in the financial district which is housed in the old Renaissance Revival Federal Reserve Bank. All rooms are comfortably furnished and equipped with every amenity. There is a fitness center with a pool, and 24-hour room service. On site are two tremendously popular French restaurants: the lavish Julien (see page 133) and Café Fleuri, as well as a delightful piano bar.

Regal Bostonian $$$-$$$$ *Faneuil Hall Marketplace, Boston, 02109; Tel: 523-3600 or 800-222-8888; Fax: 523-2454; www.millenium-hotels.com.* Overlooking the bustling Faneuil Hall Marketplace, this luxury hotel occupies two artfully restored adjoining warehouses and offers many amenities. One wing of the hotel (Bostonian) is furnished in the modern style, while the other (Harkness) is decorated in a more traditional way. Some of the hotel's 201 rooms contain fireplaces and covered balconies. Seasons, the hotel's rooftop restaurant (see page 134) is one of the best in the city.

Omni Parker House $$–$$$ *60 School Street, Boston, 02108; Tel: 227-8600; Fax: 742-5729.* Opened in 1856, this historic hotel has a lavish oak-paneled lobby with coffered ceiling. Parker's Restaurant and historic Parker's Bar are appointed with mahogany, stained glass windows, and fireplace. Some of the 552 bedrooms are small but they have all been recently renovated. 24-hour room service.

Swissotel Boston $$$ *1 Avenue de Lafayette, Tel: 451-2600 or 800-621-9200; www.swissotel.com.* Business oriented, 22-floor 501-room hotel situated in Downtown Crossing. Rooms are arranged around a central atrium and are tastefully decorated in a European style. Pool and well-equipped health club. Café Suisse, lobby bar, and 24-hour room service.

Wyndham Boston $$$-$$$$ *89 Broad Street, Boston, 02110; Tel: 556-0006; Fax: 556-0053; www.wyndham.com.* Located in the financial district in a handsome 1928 Art Deco skyscraper that underwent a $40 million dollar renovation. All 362 rooms contain the latest amenities, and marble and granite bathrooms with shower massagers. On-site fitness center. Caliterra Bar and Grille is a colorful, casual-chic dining room serving fresh Cal-Italian.

THEATER DISTRICT

Tremont House Hotel $$ *275 Tremont Street, Tel: 426-1400 or 800-331-9998.* An affordable 322 room downtown alternative. Beautifully restored historic building with coffered ceilings, marble columns, and chandeliers. Comfortable, modern rooms with coffee makers, shower massagers and irons/ironing boards. Fitness center, restaurant, and bar.

WATERFRONT

Boston Harbor Hotel $$$$ *70 Rowes Wharf, Boston, MA 02110; Tel: 439-7000 or 800-752-7077; Fax: 345-6799.* Luxurious waterfront hotel in a modern wharf building. Over half of its 230 rooms offer views of the harbor, some have balconies, and all have robes, slippers, umbrellas, flowers, and bottled water. Great brunch in the restaurant (outdoor terrace in summer). Café and bar. Fitness center and spa. Ferry service to the airport.

Boston Marriott Long Wharf $$$-$$$$ *185 State Street, Boston, MA 02109; Tel 227-0800; Fax: 227-2867.* Atrium-style hotel along the wharf with great views of the harbor. Its 400 rooms are modern and well equipped. 24-hour business center and fitness room. Indoor pool with sundeck. Two restaurants on site: Oceana (seafood) and Waves Bar and Grill (American food).

Harborside Inn $$ *185 State Street, Boston, MA 02109; Tel: 723-7500.* A small inn in a converted warehouse that is conveniently situated for Faneuil Hall. All 54 rooms are decorated in the Victorian style. Local phone calls are free. Use of exercise room and café. Complimentary continental breakfast.

BACK BAY

Boston Marriott Copley Place $$-$$$ *110 Huntington Avenue, Boston, MA 02116, Tel: (617) 236-5800; Fax: 236-5885.* A 38-floor, 1,147 room modern hotel in the Copley Place complex in the heart of Back Bay, and a half mile from the Boston Common. The stylish, frenetic atrium lobby accesses a mall with 100 shops. Well equipped rooms. 24-hour room service. Restaurant, coffee shop, cocktail lounge, indoor pool, and health club.

Boston Plaza Hotel and Towers $$-$$$$ *64 Arlington Street, Boston, MA 02116-3912; Tel: 426-2000 or 800-225-2008; Fax: 426-5545; www.bostonparkplaza.com.* A classic hotel with 960 rooms that opened in 1927 in Back Bay across from the Public Garden. It has a grand lobby, well-appointed rooms. On-site restaurants, cafes, and bars include Swan's Court, Todd's English Bonfire, Schmick's Seafood Restaurant, Montillio's Bakery and M.J. O'Connor's pub Fitness center. Business center.

Colonnade Hotel $$$-$$$$ *120 Huntington Avenue, Boston, MA 02116; Tel: 424-7000 or 800-962-3030; Fax: 424-1717; www.thecolonnadehotel.com.* A relatively small, high-style hotel that employs multilingual staff and provides outstanding personal service. Located beside symphony Hall and the Prudential Center shopping mall. 285 well-equipped guest rooms with marble bathrooms. Fitness center, outdoor roof-top pool, and 24-hour room service. On-site Brasserie Joe restaurant is a Boston favorite.

Fairmont Copley Plaza Hotel $$$$ *138 Street James Avenue, Boston, MA 02116; Tel: 800-441-1414; Fax: 375-9648; www.fairmont.com.* Mayor John F. Fitzgerald opened Boston's grand dame hotel in 1912. Its public spaces are richly embellished with carved stucco, wood paneling, marble, gilt, and mirrors. All 379 guest rooms are very comfortable, and tastefully decorated with fine reproductions. Bathrooms have extra-special amenities. 24-hour room service. The hotel's opulent décor and superb concierge service make it a favorite with presidents, celebrities, and the elite. The hotel's Oak Room restaurant is one of the best steak houses in Boston.

Copley Square Hotel $$$-$$$$ *47 Huntington Avenue, Boston, MA 02116; Tel: 536-9000 or 800-225-7062; Fax: 236-0351.* Cozy and understated Back Bay hotel with 143 rooms opened in 1891. Some of the bedrooms are on the small side, but all have modern amenities. Two restaurants: the Original Sports Saloon is a fun, popular bar serving great barbecue and 18 beers of draft, and Speeder and Earl's is popular for breakfast.

Eliot Hotel $$$-$$$$ *370 Commonwealth Avenue, Boston, MA 02115; Tel: 267-1607 or 800-44-ELIOT; Fax: 536-9114; www.eliothotel.com.* Built by the family of a

President of Harvard and adjacent to the Harvard Clubs, this elegant, all-suite hotel has offered superior European-style accommodations since 1925. All 95 suites have private pantries, marble baths, fax machines, two-line phones with data-ports, and more.

Four Seasons Hotel $$$$ *200 Boylston Street, Boston, MA 02116; Tel: 338-4400 or 800-332-3442; Fax: 423-0154.* Boston's finest hotel is a relaxed celebrity haunt overlooking the Public Garden. Antiques, handmade carpets, fresh flowers, rich woods and marble convey understated elegance throughout. It offers superb service and housekeeping. 288 comfortable rooms with fax machines, two-line phones, and little luxuries such as book lights. The Bristol Lounge is a popular piano bar and good place for relaxed afternoon tea around the hearth. Excellent health club with swimming pool and spa treatments. 24-hour concierge and room service. Business center.

Lenox Hotel $$$-$$$$ *710 Boylston Street at Copley Place, Boston, MA 02116; Tel: 536-5300 or 800-525-4800; Fax: 266-7905; www.lenoxhotel.lightband.com.* A small classic European-style hotel in Back Bay established in 1900. All 212 rooms have the latest conveniences, and corner rooms have fireplaces. Azure restaurant (sophisticated American food), City Bar (serving light fare and cocktails), and Solas pub are on site.

Midtown Hotel $–$$$ *220 Huntington Avenue, Boston, MA 02115; ; Tel: 262-1000 or 800-343-1177, Fax: 262-8739.* Motel-style accommodations conveniently located near the Convention Center and offering good value. Rooms are somewhat old fashioned in style, but equipped with phones with data ports, a hairdryer, and clock radio. Outdoor pool. Tables of Content Cafe offers breakfast. 159 rooms.

Newbury Guest House $$ *261 Newbury Street, Boston, MA 02116; Tel. (617) 437-7666; Fax: 262-4243; www.hagopianhotels.com.* Charming small hotel occupying three 1882 refurbished townhouses that are joined together and located in the heart of Back Bay. Its 32 rooms have private baths and are attractively decorated in period style. Good value. Reserve well in advance.

Ritz-Carlton Boston $$$$ *15 Arlington Street, Boston, MA 02117; Tel. (617) 536-5700 or 800-241-3333 (toll-free in US); fax (617) 536-1335.* Liveried doormen and white-gloved elevator operators set the tone at this elegant and refined hotel overlooking the Public Garden. The rooms are extremely comfortable; those in the Old Wing are the most desirable. Champagne cocktails and caviar at the club-like bar are de rigueur at this Boston institution. The dining room, lounge, and the romantic 17th-floor roof restaurant are beloved by many Bostonians. Fitness center and spa available to residents. 275 rooms.

Sheraton Hotel and Towers $$$ *39 Dalton Street, Boston, MA 02199; Tel: 236-2000 or 800-325-3535; Fax: 236-1702; www.sheraton.com.* In this twin tower 29-story hotel connected to the Hynes Convention Center and Prudential Center, standard rooms are well equipped. Lap-top high speed internet access available upon request. Apropos restaurant (featuring traditional New England Cuisine) and Turning Point Bar are both on site.

Westin Hotel $$$ *10 Huntington Avenue, Boston, MA 02116; Tel. 262-9600 or 800-WESTIN-1; fax 424-7483.* A 36-story 800 room tower connected to Copley Place shopping center. Rooms are equipped with the very latest amenities – coffee maker, iron/ironing board, two line speakerphone with data port, and more. The hotel has three restaurants: Turner Fisheries Restaurant and Oyster Bar, Bar 10 (Mediterranean cuisine), and the legendary Palm Restaurant (savory steaks). Fitness center with pool. 24-hour room service.

THE SOUTH END

Chandler Inn $-$$ *26 Chandler Street, Boston, MA 02116; Tel: 482-3450 or 800-842-3450; Fax: 542-3428; www.chandlerinn.com.* A 56-room inn located in the center of the city. Private baths, direct dial telephones, and color televisions. Largely gay guests, but all are welcome. Very helpful and friendly staff. The rooms are fairly basic, but comfortable and offer dataports, irons, and satellite television service.

CAMBRIDGE

Cambridge House Bed & Breakfast Inn $–$$$ *2218 Massachusetts Avenue, Cambridge, MA 02138; Tel: 491-6300 or 800-232-9989; Fax: 868-2848; www.cambridgehouse.com.* Lovely, restored 1892 Greek Revival house with elaborate but comfortable rooms decorated in Victorian style. Many of its 16 rooms have four-poster beds, and two have working fireplaces. Full breakfast and evening buffet included. No smoking.

Charles Hotel $$$-$$$$ *1 Bennett Street, Cambridge, MA 02138; Tel: 864-1200 or 800-882-1818; Fax: 864-5717; www.charleshotel.com.* An oasis of peace and luxury right in the center of Cambridge. Stylishly modern establishment with attentive staff and 296 rooms. Chic, attractive bedrooms with such amenities as Bose wave radios, three dual-line phones, bathroom TV and scale, and umbrellas. Henrietta's Table is a highly rated restaurant, and the

Regattabar is a fabulous jazz club. 24-hour room service, health club with pool.

Harvard Square Hotel $$ *110 Mount Auburn Street, Cambridge, MA 02138; Tel: 864-5200 or 800-458-5886; Fax: 864-2409.* A four-story modern hotel with 73 rooms that are appointed with items such as hairdryers, umbrellas, and phones with data ports. It's well run and just a few steps from Harvard Square. Café. Free parking.

The Inn at Harvard $$$ *1201 Massachusetts Avenue, Cambridge, MA 02138; Tel: 491-2222 or 800-458-5886; Fax: 520-3711; www.theinnatharvard.com.* In Harvard Square adjacent to Harvard Yard this small modern urban inn offers 113 rooms furnished with well-lit desks, two telephone with data ports, bathrobes, and other amenities. They are arranged around a comfortable four-story atrium lounge that incorporates literary and work areas. It's furnished in traditional New England style. Atrium Dining Room serves New England f*are.*

University Park Hotel $$-$$$ *MIT 20 Sidney Street, Cambridge, MA 02139; Tel: 577-0200; www.hotel@mit.com.* A unique accommodation located at MIT, whose contemporary décor includes robots from the MIT Artificial Intelligence Lab which grace the lobby. All rooms include complimentary high-speed Internet access, ergonomically designed furniture, Sony PlayStations, two-line portable telephones, and data ports. Exercise Room. 24-hour room service. Sidney's Grille restaurant serves American-style food in a funky atmosphere.

Recommended Restaurants

Reservations are recommended at most places for dinner, unless they have a no-reservations policy, which will mean a wait, sometimes an hour or more.

The price ranges below indicate the cost of a three-course dinner, excluding drinks, tax, and service. Lunch is considerably cheaper than dinner; prix fixe menus are also good value.

$$$$	above $50
$$$	above $40–$50
$$	$25–$40
$	under $25

BEACON HILL

Beacon Hill Bistro $ *25 Charles Street; Tel: 888-959-2442*, Serving breakfast, lunch and dinner daily. www.beaconhill-hotel.com. Located in the heart of Beacon Hill, this intimate small hotel has twelve tasteful guest rooms.

.

Figs $–$$ *42 Charles Street; Tel. 742-3447. Dinner daily.* Specialty pizzas are why the crowds come to this warm casual spot although there's more — pastas, *risotto*, and salads — in the repertoire. Toppings are original — figs and *prosciutto*, or shrimp and basil *aioli*.

Hungry i $$ *7-½ Charles Street; Tel. (617) 227-3524. Lunch Tues–Fri and Sun; Dinner Tues–Sun.* A romantic subterranean dining room with a countrified air established by warm red-brick walls, fresh flowers, and fine china. In winter the fire makes it even more appealing. Fine cuisine.

Lala Rockh $–$$ *97 Mt. Vernon Street; Tel. 720-5511. Dinner daily.* This Persian restaurant is named after an epic romance. Its ambiance is enhanced by low-ceilings, miniatures, calligraphy, and other Persian artifacts. The cuisine is fragrant with cumin, saffron, mint, basil, and other spices and herbs combined in stews, kebab dishes. Delights include dishes such as saffron-seared chicken in a light tomato broth with rice perfumed with cumin, cinnamon, and rose petals.

DOWNTOWN AND FINANCIAL DISTRICT

Julien $$ *Le Meridien Hotel, 250 Franklin Street; Tel. 451-1900 or 800-543-4300. Dinner daily.* Boston's most beautiful dining room (gilded coffered ceiling, wingback chairs) serving lavish contemporary French cuisine. Expect caviar, *foie gras*, and truffles, and excellent European dishes.

Lock-Ober $$$ *3 Winter Place (between Washington and Tremont); Tel: 542-1340. Lunch Mon–Fri; Dinner Mon–Sat.* A Boston tradition since 1875, at least for gentlemen – women were only admitted to the Men's Café 20 years ago. Carved paneling, stained glass, white linen, cigar smoke, old-fashioned steaks and continental cuisine. Jacket and tie required for men.

Radius $$$$ *8 High Street; Tel.426-1234. Lunch Mon–Fri; Dinner Mon–Sat.* A stark minimalist dark-gray dining room attracting a power-lunch and dinner crowd. The modern French cuisine uses flavored oils and light reductions — pork in a cumin jus, halibut with red pepper syrup. Sinful deserts that shouldn't be missed. Extensive French–Californian wine list.

Seasons $$$$ *Regal Bostonian Hotel, Faneuil Hall Marketplace, corner of North and Blackstone streets; Tel. 523-4119. Breakfast daily; Lunch Mon–Fri; Dinner Mon–Sat.* Spacious dining room overlooking Faneuil Hall Marketplace offers gracious contemporary American cuisine. Great fish and such winners as beef tenderloin with a port wine sauce or citrus- and herb-glazed duck in game jus. Good cheeses and extensive wine list.

Ye Olde Union Oyster House $-$$ *41 Union Street (near Government Center); Tel. 227-2750. 11am–9:30 Mon–Thur, Sun; 11am–10pm Fri, Sat.* Boston's oldest restaurant, established in 1826. Wooden booths and shucking bars make for great atmospheric. Oysters are always a good choice.

THEATER DISTRICT

Brew Moon $-$$ *115 Stuart Street; Tel: 523-6467. Lunch and dinner daily.* Sleek modern microbrewery serving saloon classics like buffalo wings, beer-battered onion rings, plus some innovative, often spicy cuisine.

Jacob Wirth $ *31 Stuart Street; Tel. (617) 338-8586. Lunch and dinner daily (closes 8pm Sun and Mon).* Traditional German fare — *bratwurst, knockwurst, sauerbraten, wiener schnitzel*, and potato pancakes. Good choice of beers in splendid historic bar. Second oldest restaurant in Boston.

THE NORTH END

Daily Catch $$ *323 Hanover Street; Tel.523-8567. Sun–Thurs 11:30am–10pm; Fri–Sat 11:30am–11pm.* Calamari cooked 10 different ways, plus swordfish, tuna, salmon. Tiny, fun, and always packed (expect a wait).

Mamma Maria's Ristorante $ *3 North Square; (at Prince and North Streets), Tel: 523-0077. 5–10pm Mon–Thur, Sun; 5–11pm Fri, Sat.* Fine Northern Italian cuisine served in a classic, romantic little upstairs dining room away from the hubbub of Hanover Street. Osso buco, grilled meats, and fish of the day plus stellar pasta dishes.

Terramia $$–$$$ *98 Salem Street; Tel: 523-3112. Dinner daily.* One of the small restaurants that has been raising the reputation of the North End. It offers a limited number of pastas and risottos plus such updated American-Italian dishes as roasted pork tenderloin in a pepper and dried California prune sauce.

Trattoria A Scalinatella $–$$ 253 Hanover Street, Tel: 742-8240. Dinner daily. Homemade pastas, tantalizing fish and meat specials, and a fine wine list. A delightful choice for fine food and a great night out.

WATERFRONT

Anthony's Pier 4 $$ *140 Northern Avenue; Tel: (617) 423-6363. Lunch and dinner daily.* A famous seafood restaurant, with fabulous Harbor views that has welcomed everyone from Liz Taylor to George Bush. Chowders, lobsters, and broiled, baked, grilled, or poached seafood. Steaks for the unconvinced. Book ahead.

Aura $-$$ *1 Seaport Lane (Seaport Hotel); Tel: 385-4300. 6:30–2:30pm, 5:30–10:30 pm daily.* Creative American fare served in an out of the way location. Its delectable deserts cannot disappoint. Reservations recommended.

BACK BAY AND THE FENWAY

Aujourd'hui $$$$ *Four Seasons Hotel, 200 Boylston Street; Tel. 351-2071. 6:30–11pm, 11:30am–2pm Mon–Fri; 7–12pm Sat–Sun.; 5:30–10pm Mon–Sun.* A premier restaurant. Plush fabrics, wood paneling, and views of the Public Gardens are the backdrop for superb cuisine featuring caviar, foie gras, and dishes cooked in flavorful jus and reductions. Fabulous if pricey brunch. Reservations recommended.

Clio $$$ *The Eliot Hotel, 370A Commonwealth Avenue; Tel. 536-7200.;Dinner Tues–Thurs & Sun 5:30–10pm; Fri–Sat 5:30–10:30pm; Breakfast daily from 7am.* Lavish supper club setting with mohair banquettes and leopard skin carpeting where award-winning chef Kenneth Oringer serves up delicacies such as Salmon with red ginger vinaigrette, roasted duck with kumquats, and Jerusalem artichoke soup nightly.

Elephant Walk $$ *9900 Beacon Street (Park Drive); Tel: 247-1500. Lunch: 11:30am–2:30pm Mon–Fri; Dinner: 5pm–10pm Sun–Thurs, 5pm–11pm Fri & Sat.* Superb French-Cambodian restaurant which is extremely popular.

L'Espalier $$$$ *30 Gloucester Street (at Newbury Street); Tel. (617) 262-3023. Dinner Mon–Sat.* Arguably the best restaurant in town. Located in an elegant Victorian townhouse it provides superb service and sublime nominally French (but really contemporary fusion) cuisine featuring organic ingredients and intense flavors, often derived from multi-layered broths. Signature dishes include the mushroom soup, and chicken coated in *mole* with a *tomatillo* sauce. Don't miss the molten-centered chocolate fondant cake. Excellent cheese selection. Great wine list. First-rate vegetarian menu too.

Jae's Café & Grill $$ *212 Stuart Street (at Arlington); Tel. (617) 451-7788 Lunch and dinner daily.* A popular place that is always crowded with boisterous patrons enjoying the Pan Asian cuisine. There are noodle and rice dishes, "designer rolls" (sushi-style), Korean specialties plus dishes like grilled salmon with jalapeno salsa.

Legal Sea Foods $$ *35 Columbus Avenue; Tel: 426-7777. Serving lunch and dinner from 11am–11pm daily.* A member of the highly successful and dependable chain that delivers good, fresh seafood in an ambiance of polished wood and brass. Two favorites are the coconut shrimp with orange-ginger sauce and the lobster bake. The fresh fish can be cooked in any style you want – Cajun or jerk style, with a spicy.

The Ritz-Carlton Boston Dining Room $$$$ *Ritz-Carlton Boston Hotel, 15 Arlington Street; Tel. 536-5700. Brunch Sun; Dinner Mon–Sat.* Contemporary American-international cuisine served in sumptuous surroundings (gilded columns, drapes, and cobalt-blue chandeliers) overlooking the Public Gardens. Super-fresh ingredients are used to make such intensely flavored dishes as striped bass in a peppercorn sauce with corn, chanterelle, and preserved lemon, or braised rabbit with forest mushrooms and duck liver. Good cheese selection and spectacular fruit salad. Reservations essential.

Turner Fisheries $$ *Westin Hotel, Copley Place, 10 Huntington Avenue; Tel. 424-7425. Lunch and dinner daily.* Top-notch straightforward seafood and some of the best chowder in the city in spite of the modern and antiseptic surroundings. Raw bar and jazz bar add to the ambiance.

Vox Populi $-$$ *755 Boylston Street (between Exeter and Fairfield Streets); Tel: 424-8300; Mon–Fri 11:30am–10pm; Sat–Sun 11:30am–3pm & 3pm–10pm.* Innovative, affordable food in a stylish, relaxed atmosphere. Great spot for people watching.

SOUTH END

Aquitaine $$ *569 Tremont Street (at Clarendon Street); Tel. 424-8577. Dinner from Sun–Wed 5:30pm–10pm & Thu–Sat 5:30pm–11pm;* Brunch Sat & Sun 10am–3pm. Sleek, dark and woody interior. Try the Hanger steak flavored with truffle demiglace and fries.

Hamersley's Bistro $$$ *Tremont Street; Tel. 423-2700. Serving dinner nightly; Dinner Sun 5:30–9:30pm, Mon–Fri 6–10 pm, Sat 5:30–10:30 pm.* A winning bistro serving contemporary and inventive cuisine. Select from main courses like lemon-peppered duck with wild mushrooms and red wine sauce, seared scallops, and tuna tartare with lemon-mint vinaigrette.

CHINATOWN

Chau Chow $ *52 Beach Street; Tel. 338-8158; Dim sum: daily 8am–3pm; Lunch: daily 11am–3pm; Dinner: 3pm–4am.* Longtime favorite for good Chinese, especially seafood and dim sum at great prices.

Ginza $$ *16 Hudson Street (between Beach and Kneeland streets); Tel. 338-2261. Lunch and dinner Mon–Sun 11:30–2 am.* Go for the best sushi in town – 50 varieties.

Penang $ *685 Washington Street; Tel. 451-6373. Daily 11:30am–11:30pm.* Casual, popular Malaysian restaurant with bamboo accents. Plenty of rice and noodle dishes plus good spicy casseroles made with shrimp or beef and dishes reflecting Indian, Thai, and Singaporean roots.

Pho Pasteur $ *682 Washington Street; Tel. (617) 482-7467. Lunch and dinner daily.* Very popular plain Vietnamese restaurant where you can make a meal of a hearty noodle soup or choose among the traditional Vietnamese dishes.

CAMBRIDGE, CHARLESTOWN, AND SOMERVILLE

Border Café $ *32 Church Street, Harvard Square; Tel. 864-6100; Sun–Thu 11–1am; Fri–Sat 11–2am.* This Tex-Mex restaurant is one of Cambridge's busiest young hangouts. Expect a long wait, and look forward to wooden tables, margaritas, and large portions of decent Mexican food.

Dali $$ *415 Washington Street (at Beacon Street), Somerville; Tel. 661-3254. Dinner nightly 5:30–11pm.* Out-of-the-way, authentic, and fun Spanish restaurant, famous for its more than 30 tapas (anchovies/black olives on tomato toast; pork sausage with figs). Seafood, meat, and game dishes too including classic *paella.* Warm ambience with pretty tile, braided garlic and peppers, plus an exotic washing line.

East Coast Grill $$ *1271 Cambridge Street (at Prospect Street), Inman Square; Tel. 491-6568. Dinner Sun–Thur 5:30–10pm, Fri–Sat 5:30–10:30pm; Brunch Sun 11am–2:30pm.* Superb barecue and spicy Caribbean food washed down with daiquiris and fabulous margaritas in a noisy, cramped, and extremely busy dining room. Expect a long wait.

Henrietta's Table $$–$$$ *Charles Hotel, 1 Bennett Street, Harvard Square, Cambridge; Tel. 661-5005. Mon–Fri 6:30–11am, Sat 7–11:30am, Sun 7–10:30am; Mon–Sat 12–3pm; Dinner Sun–Thur 5:30–10pm, Fri–Sat 5:30–11pm; Sat Brunch 12 –3pm, Sun Brunch 11:30 am–2:30pm.* Much loved by the Cambridge intelligentsia who appreciate the reasonably priced food and Shaker farmhouse-style ambiance.

$$Miracle of Science Bar & Grill $-$$ *321 Massachusetts Avenue, Cambridge; Tel: 868-2866.* Comfortable, ultra-modern space, a favorite with MIT students. Good beer and American food. Drinks are served in laboratory beakers.

Olives $$$ *10 City Square, Charlestown; Tel. 242-1999; 5:30–10pm Mon–Thur; 5:30–10:15pm Fri; 5–10:15pm Sat.* Bostonians flock to savor Mediterranean cuisine and the dishes that emerge from the brick oven and wood grill. Wonderful pasta, meat, and fish dishes such as wood-grilled sea bass served over horseradish mashed potatoes with green beans, bacon, and lobster salad vinaigrette. Expect long waits.

Rosebud Diner $ *381 Summer street, Somerville; Tel: 666-6015. 8am–11pm Sun–Thur; 8am–midnight Fri & Sat.* Traditional American diner food served in a 1941 restored dining car. A delicious step back through time.

Salts $$ *798 Main Street, Cambridge; Tel. 876-8444. Dinner Tues–Sun 5:30–10:30pm.* Small brightly colored bistro where the salt is indeed proudly displayed and the cuisine is wowing Boston foodies. Expect grilled salmon in a smoked bacon vinaigrette, or roast duckling scented with cinnamon and served with caramelized clementines over chestnut lima bean stew.

INDEX